MILESTONES & MIRACLES

By
Marcia Mitchell

Light House Publications
Tulsa, Oklahoma

Other Scripture references are taken from the following versions:
King James Version (KJV)
Revised Standard Version (RSV)
New King James Version (NKJV)

By the author's request, all proceeds from the sales of this book will benefit The Little Light House, Inc.

Milestones and Miracles

Printed in Canada

ISBN Paperback: 978-0-9635709-1-8

Cover illustration by: Terry Dugan Design

Dedication

Dedicated
to my heavenly Father who
authored the stories penned herein
and lovingly gave me a second
chance to share them with my world. . . .

. . . and to God's special children
who continue to
inspire and teach
all those
whose hearts are willing
to listen. . . .

. . . and to Sheryl
whose child-like faith
moved me
to dare to believe God for
the miracle of The Little Light House.

Acknowledgments

To my husband, Phil –
For your understanding, encouragement, and most of all, your unconditional love. Without it, this book could never have taken form. You are my one, true love and best friend.

To my daughter, Missy –
For allowing God to masterfully use your life to affect many! For being my greatest cheerleader during this writing. I love you, darlin'!

To my dear friend Alma –
For your vision for this book. For your belief in God's ability to write it through me. For your steadfast friendship and invaluable encouragement. And for serving as God's instrument to help bring this story into print. I'll *always* treasure you in my heart.

To Norma Jean Lutz –
For the time, energy and heart you poured into this project. For believing with me that this story needed to be told and helping me to tell it. For the volumes you taught me. Thank you and God bless you!

To countless others –
Whose lives may not be recorded on the pages of this book, but were definitely used by God as He unfolded the milestones and miracles of The Little Light House.

LIST OF CREDITS

Typing: Debbie Hedges
Photography: Herald Givens
Research: Lois Zellner
Artistic Contribution: Jennith Moncrief
Technical and Administrative Assistance:
Jean Winfrey
Reviewers: Sherrie Hull, Tammy Gill, Mary Phillips, Linda Dunham, Mike Brady, Tom Lawson and Donald Shamblin, PhD.

Welcome

For many of us, when we recognize a need, it is natural to delay our response, or to ignore the need altogether. But what if your awareness of a need is actually God speaking to your heart? What if God is calling you to join him in meeting the needs around you? What if he is inviting you to change the world?

Inside these pages is the story of an extraordinary ministry designed to meet the needs of children with special needs. But on a higher level, it is a story of obedience, faith, and determination. It is a story full of challenges that require more endurance than any human can walk out on their own. It is a story of complete dependence on God. And of God's unfailing faithfulness to those who fully trust him.

In each of our journeys, there will be doubters, cheerleaders, and co-laborers. There will be an enemy, constantly scattering seeds of doubt. Most importantly, there will be a God of love and faithfulness who will carry out his plans and purposes as we continue to seek his face.

Whether you are reading this story for an historical perspective of the ministry, or you find yourself on your own journey of faith, we hope this story inspires you to respond to God's calling on your life. May you be strengthened and encouraged by this true account of modern-day miracles.

Kim Burnett
LLH Board Chair, 2017-2020

Contents

Foreword by Michael Allen Brady xi

Preface xiii

1 Why, Lord? 1

2 Prayers, Perfume and Piggyback Rides 7

3 Miracle Morning 13

4 What Next, Lord? 17

5 But God Can! 21

6 A Dream Embraced 27

7 Rainbow Dreams, Miracle Realities 31

8 The Little White Schoolhouse 39

9 Kristi's Calling 45

10 Colors That Smell and Bumps That Spell 47

11 Appointed, Anointed and Equipped 53

12 Divine Requisitions 59

13 God's Blueprints 65

14 A Lesson in Faith 73

15 The Donut Miracle 77

16 Cream Off the Top 81

17 Where Are You, Lord? 87

18 Tightening Our Budget and Stretching Our Faith 93

19 Without Words, They Teach 101

20	When There's No Answer – Don't Hang Up!	105
21	And a Full Tummy Sure Helps!	111
22	The Fleece	115
23	God Moves in Mysterious Ways	123
24	Angels Unaware	127
25	God's Economy	131
26	Promised Land	137
27	Master Coordinator	147
28	State-of-the-*Heart* Curriculum	157
Epilogue		161

Foreword

Following a solo recital in New York City, the great pianist, Van Cliburn, was signing autographs and making small talk with his radiant admirers. Near the end of the line, a lady clutching his hands said to him, "I'd give my life to be able to play like that!"

Van Cliburn looked back at her with steady eyes and simply said, "Madame, I have."

Was his simple, three-word answer merely a quip intended for self-elevation at her expense? Or was the grand master, seasoned by a life of tireless dedication and single-mindedness, speaking directly to her heart with equal measures of challenge and encouragement?

Perhaps she also heard what I think he intended: "You could do as well, if you were to commit the same level of dedication and obedience to a single calling, forsaking all distractions, until you are able to play the piece with the full range of gentleness, grace, enthusiasm and strength intended by the composer himself."

Maybe you have been like this woman — full of admiration for the works of others, yet deaf to the beautiful music God has called and equipped you to play in a different concert hall. Or, maybe you are more like a seasoned pianist who grows tired of the performance and begins to question his very calling.

This book, which is written by a woman considered by many to be one of God's grand masters of dedication and obedience, offers the same challenge and encouragement, but with an indispensable added ingredient — faith in God and reliance on His promises.

Marcia Mitchell, Executive Director and Co-Founder of The Little Light House, would be the first to agree that without child-like faith, this ministry to children would not be possible. She would also point out that while there have been times of loneliness, she has never been alone. Rather than a solo performance, you will see that God more often prefers a full concert under the direction of a trusted conductor with her back to the audience. With obedient leadership, the individual musicians come and go, adding their gifts and talents with strings, percussion and brass, producing a far-more-dramatic result than could be possible with one grand master, playing alone.

The Little Light House has been the stage for one continuous performance of God's miracles and acts of love for over twenty years. It has been one of my greatest joys to have been there for a few of the acts. It is an even greater joy to know that the Composer himself is still writing the music, and that the love and the joy continue.

— Michael Allen Brady
Past Board Chairman
The Little Light House
Tulsa, Oklahoma

Preface

It was the spring of 1988. A health problem I had been living with for some time seemed to be worsening.

An unbearable tiredness had crept up on me, at times robbing me of my energy to such an extent that I found myself unable to walk even the shortest of distances.

Finally, one morning, limp with fatigue, I called our family doctor, hoping he could provide an immediate remedy. Too weak to drive, I called Mary, my close friend and neighbor, and asked if she would drive me to his office nearby. We arrived there in minutes.

Even so, by the time I reached his office, I was hyperventilating and I soon lost consciousness. Moments later, I was being transported by ambulance to the nearest hospital. By the time I arrived at the emergency room, my ears were filled with rushing sounds. Tingling sensations progressed through my arms and legs.

Images and thoughts floated in and out of my consciousness. There was a flurry of activity — blood samples to be taken, questions to answer and forms to sign. My husband and my seventeen-year-old daughter were notified, and they rushed to the hospital to be at my side. The doctor advised them of my need for emergency surgery.

All too soon I felt the rhythmical jarring of gurney wheels as orderlies rushed me through the corridors toward the operating room. White squares of acoustical ceiling blurred past overhead.

As I was being transferred to the surgical table, the reality of the moment hit me. With any surgery there is always an element of risk. What if — what if I don't survive the surgery? The thought sent an icy chill through my body.

The nurses and technicians continued with their preparations. My mind raced as I took stock of my life. My reflections brought me a measure of peace — until I remembered the book God had commissioned me to write many years before. It had never been written. My heart began to race. If something happened to me now, it would never be written. The miraculous stories would never be told; the lessons would never be shared.

Even worse, I saw myself standing empty-handed before God, knowing there was no one left to write it. I found myself beseeching Him, "Please, Lord, please bring me through this. And this time, I *will* write your book. I'll tell of your miracles, I'll share your principles. I'll *make* time. I promise." My thoughts melted into fuzziness as I succumbed to the effects of the anesthetic.

A few hours later, I awoke with the inexpressible joy that always accompanies the grace of God. I had been granted a second chance, and the privilege of fulfilling my promise.

The book you now hold in your hands is that fulfillment. It is dedicated to an all-loving God whose mercy is everlasting and whose grace endures forever!

> Publish his glorious acts throughout the earth. Tell everyone about the amazing things he does. For the Lord is great beyond description, and greatly to be praised. (Psalms 96:3-4a)

1
Why, Lord?

The dulling effect of the anesthetic slowly began to subside. The warmth of the heated blanket felt good as I roused into a conscious awareness of where I was. Quiet activity filled the recovery room. Attendants wheeled groggy patients in from surgery, leaving them in the care of nurses who skillfully monitored their vital signs and gently coaxed them back to consciousness.

The tender voice of a nearby nurse sounded familiar to me. I strained to focus. From across the room, I caught a glimpse of a pretty, petite blonde with sensitive blue eyes. It pleased me to see that Donna, a friend from church, was working the day shift. In a moment, she was at my side. She was as surprised to see me as I was to see her. I was still feeling a bit hazy as she gently covered me with fresh, warm blankets, but I managed to recount to her the events that had led up to my emergency surgery.

Her gentle manner and tender compassion reminded me of another time when nurses had ministered soothing words of comfort in the very same hospital seventeen years before. Soon Donna was called away, leaving me to my memories. . . .

* * *

My mind raced back over those seventeen years. Phil and I had been married over three years when I finally became pregnant. We were jubilant! From the start, I had wanted a baby girl, and for the duration of the pregnancy, I dreamed of nothing else. I could see her in my mind's eye, pretty and pink and covered from head to toe with ribbons and lace!

On August 11, 1970, at 11:59 PM, the obstetrician finally announced, "It's a girl!"

Unable to contain my exuberance, I laughed with delight. When the nurse brought her closer for me to see, I was completely overcome with joy! Truly, she was beyond even my greatest fantasies! Her hair was the blondest I had ever seen; in fact, it was actually white! The nurses evidently agreed because they immediately nicknamed her "Little Snow White." She was extraordinarily fair from head to toe, almost Dresden-like. Of course, Phil and I had each been light-skinned and blonde as children. My heart wanted to nestle into the comfort of my reasoning, but my mind was unsettled.

Something stirred within me. Hesitantly, I asked the doctor, "Is she all right?"

The doctor's answer remains with me to this day: "She's as perfect as you would want her to be." His soothing words calmed my anxiety.

Finally, I was taken back to my room. Phil was there to greet me with a countenance that blended pride with exhaustion. We had a few wonderful moments together and finalized our decision to name our precious new baby, Michelle Louise. With a grin, Phil said, "But we'll call her Missy, okay?"

Shortly before he left, I gathered the courage to ask Phil if he felt anything might be wrong with her. He assured me she was fine and gently reminded me of my tendency to worry needlessly. He gave me a tender kiss and slipped quietly out the door.

He returned the next morning, just as he had promised. He was in the best of spirits, still the epitome of a proud, new father! Moments later, the pediatrician arrived. Looking a bit too solemn, he spoke softly, "I guess you both know you have a very special baby."

"Of course she's special!" I quickly responded, bursting with pride. That a pediatrician, who saw so many children, would comment that our child was exceptional caused both Phil and me to spill over with delight. But the doctor's tone became more serious.

"I don't think you understand. You see, your baby is very special because babies *like* her are extremely rare – only one in 50,000. She was born with a condition known as albinism, which results in a lack of pigment in the hair, skin, and eyes. Her vision is also affected but it will be several years before you'll know the degree of vision she has. At best, she will be *legally blind.* I'm afraid it's non-correctable." His voice grew distant. Though he continued on, I didn't hear anything else he said. My heart and mind had locked in on one word – *blind!*

Phil saw the pediatrician to the door, and as he did so, tears began to sting my eyes. No! It can't be true! Surely the doctor must be wrong. But other doctors confirmed his diagnosis.

In the following days, Phil seemed pensive. As for me, I cried for hours as the same question echoed over and over in my head. "Why, Lord? *Why* have you done this to us? *How* could you do this to us?"

Several days passed. Then one particular day, Phil was late for his regular visit. When he finally arrived, I was anxious to know why he had been so delayed. His evasiveness heightened my curiosity all the more. Stumbling over his words, he attempted to explain.

"On the way to the hospital," he began, "I couldn't help wondering. What if things turn out for the worst? What if Missy can't see at all? Or, what if she can see, but can't see well enough to. . . ." He hesitated a moment as he stared out the window, ". . . to see a bird in flight, or the stars, or –."

I waited for him to collect his thoughts. "I couldn't stop thinking about it, and so I just kept driving," he explained. "I studied the landscape and everything my eyes could absorb. I noticed how blue the sky was – clear, with only a few white, wispy clouds."

He moved from the window, back to my bedside. "I began to wonder how we might describe it all to her. I tried to think of words to capture it all. That's when I noticed the grass. Marcia, for the first time, I realized that grass isn't simply a green mass. It's millions upon millions of tiny, individual blades! Even though I was looking at things I've seen every day of my life, it was as though I was seeing it all for the first time. As though through Missy, I've been given a rare gift – a new look at our world!"

I took my eyes off of him for a moment and looked at the roses by my bedside. As I studied them, they seemed to take on an added brilliance. I wondered – is this part of the answer to my questions? Is God trying to help us understand the "why" of all this?

Through Missy's imperfect vision — is He trying to teach *us* how to truly see?

* * *

A voice seemed to be coming from far, far away. "Mother, how are you feeling?" Missy's soft voice gently drew me back to the present from my reflections of so many years ago. The surgery was over. I'd been moved from recovery and was in my own room. Phil and Missy were by my side. Missy looked unusually pretty with her soft, white hair framing her delicate, seventeen-year-old features. She gazed down at me with searching, pale-blue eyes.

Oh, Missy, I thought without speaking, has it really been seventeen years since I lay in this hospital, cradling you in my arms? So much has happened during those years!

How could I have known then that God would work through your life to unfold an entire ministry and do so much more? Had I really asked "Why?" the day after you were born? I had indeed. And that same day God began to answer. And, almost two decades later, He continues to reveal divine revelations to the very same question!

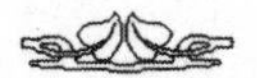

> As he was walking along, he saw a man blind from birth. "Master," his disciples asked him, "why was this man born blind? Was it a result of his own sins or those of his parents?" "Neither," Jesus answered. *"But to demonstrate the power of God."* (John 9:1-3, italics mine)

2
Prayers, Perfume and Piggyback Rides

Looking back, it is evident God was guiding and providing from the day Missy was born.

Following her birth, she and I were detained at the hospital longer than normal. A kidney infection complicated my recovery, but finally I was well enough to be discharged.

Feeling some anxiety about leaving the security of the knowledgeable physicians, Phil and I asked if they could offer us any advice. We were eager to take our newborn home, yet giving birth to a baby with "special needs" had also given birth within us to strong feelings of inadequacy. We were at a loss to know how to teach a baby with a visual impairment, or how to help her develop.

Because of my background in education and some exposure to blind individuals during my life, I was somewhat aware of the challenges involved in helping a visually impaired baby develop normally. I knew that eighty-five percent of all learning takes place visually. I also knew how critical the early childhood years are to the learning process.

The words of the well-meaning doctors will always remain with us. "Take her home, love her and treat her like a normal child," they casually advised. But how could we? We didn't know how much she could see – or *if* she could see at all.

We attempted to put our fears aside and for the time being to focus on the first part of their guidance: "Take her home and love her."

Loving her was easy. Angelic in appearance, she had a rim of glistening white hair which formed a kind of halo effect around her head. To make sure everyone knew we had a baby girl, I kept a bow taped to the top of her head at all times. Then, too, while still an infant, she was fitted with dark glasses to protect her light-sensitive eyes. She was quite a sight, always covered with lace and bows and, of course, her shades!

As the weeks passed, while we delighted in Missy, we also grew increasingly concerned about her development. She wasn't progressing as rapidly as other babies her age, and when we smiled at her, she didn't smile back. Already she was lagging behind, developmentally.

We lacked adequate training to teach her, and yet there were no centers or preschools in our local area that offered the assistance we so desperately needed. My fear turned into chronic worry.

Weeks passed. Missy continued to fall behind in her development. My worrying increased. Surely there had to be ways we could help her learn. Then one day, I remembered something my mother had consistently repeated to me when I was a child: "Marcia, don't worry so much – just pray!"

Perhaps God would hear our prayers and send us help and guidance in teaching and helping our child.

So we prayed and asked the Lord to help us in our dilemma.

A short time later, we learned about a place in Oklahoma City called The Child Study Center. The city was a little more than an hour's drive from Tulsa. The center's staff, we were told, consisted of a physician, social workers and special education teachers who worked with deaf and blind infants and children. We quickly wrote and asked if they would consider helping us.

A month passed and we had still received no word from the center. Throughout the waiting period, I worried about the fact that Missy wasn't deaf! I feared they wouldn't take her because she was only visually impaired.

Phil was undone! "Marcia! Who ever heard of worrying over the fact that your child isn't deaf?" he teased. Then again, he understood all too well. We both felt so very desperate and the one program available served *only* children who were *both* deaf and blind.

⋆ ⋆ ⋆

Christmas of that year brought us an unexpected sense of joy and relief when we discovered Missy did have some degree of vision. We arrived home late one evening. We had left the Christmas lights on which outlined the windows of our home. I was stepping up to the front door, cradling Missy in my arms, when I realized her eyes were beholding the multi-colored lights!

It took little intuition on the part of her daddy and me to know that she was seeing. To what extent, we wouldn't know for years, but we did know we could never have received a greater Christmas gift than the knowledge that our little girl had some degree of vision.

To celebrate, Missy's grandma and grandpa brought her a miniature Christmas tree covered with tiny twinkling lights! To this day, Christmas lights remind us of the precious gift of sight, and we cherish the tradition they hold.

Soon after Christmas, our joy was increased when we were given an appointment to go to the center in Oklahoma City. We dressed Missy in her best pink frills and made it a family trip. The staff was warm and friendly and quickly put us at ease. Missy was evaluated and we were interviewed. In the final analysis, they decided Missy was too young, at five months old, to accurately test her hearing. Consequently they assumed she was deaf until they could prove otherwise! On that basis she was admitted into their program.

There was no doubt about it. I knew God had opened those doors! I soon came to realize that Missy's hearing was better than mine! Often, when I was feeding her, she would suddenly stop eating, tilt her head and listen intently. I would stop and listen, too. Then, and only then, would I hear an airplane, or an ambulance, or perhaps a car door closing in the driveway.

The center placed our family on a "Home Program" through which parents are taught how to work with their child. It was exactly what we had prayed for. We were starved for knowledge, and they immediately began to instruct us.

At the outset, they asked if Missy was a good baby. "Remarkably so," we proudly replied. They glanced at one another with concern.

"Is she quite content to be left alone in her crib or playpen for long periods of time?"

"Oh, yes!" we responded. As we did so, we began to sense their concern.

"You need to get Missy on your back," the instructor explained. "Carry her in a carrier, piggyback-style, for as long as possible during the day. In this way she will have countless learning experiences she wouldn't have otherwise." She went on to explain that while Missy might seem happier and feel more secure in the familiar territory of her crib, she wasn't learning in that limited environment. It was better for her to be up and about so she could receive the maximum amount of stimulation to enhance her development.

When we returned home, we couldn't wait to follow through on their suggestions. Alone one morning, I realized how much Missy had absorbed from simply implementing their piggyback idea. Having her on my back so that she could experience *her* world made *me* more aware of *her* world as well! As I fixed breakfast, I realized she could *smell* the bacon frying. She could *feel* the cold from the refrigerator door opening and closing, and the heat from the oven as I pulled out warm biscuits.

Later, as I made the bed, I realized she was being made aware of how my posture was changing as I moved about. I also discovered she could feel the vibrations in my back as I spoke. All day long, she was learning, sensing and discovering — all from a piggyback ride!

Phil and I had been further advised to decide on a particular kind of cologne or perfume and to wear it all the time. This practice enabled Missy to always know when we were near.

We laughed as we thought about how our friends as well could tell when we were coming, because we were always doused with the same kinds of perfume and cologne. But being assured Missy could identify us made it well worthwhile.

There were countless other enlightening suggestions made by the caring professionals at the center. We tried each suggestion they offered. And as we did so, we watched Missy progress. Months later, to our delight, she was functioning on a normal developmental level.

The piggyback rides and the perfume, along with all the other guidance we'd received, had contributed to her remarkable progress. And we rejoiced! But most of all we rejoiced to know that our prayers had been answered. For with those answered prayers came assurance about the future.

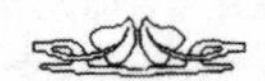

> Don't worry about anything; instead, pray about everything; tell God your needs and don't forget to thank him for his answers. If you do this you will experience God's peace, which is far more wonderful than the human mind can understand. His peace will keep your thoughts and your hearts quiet and at rest as you trust in Christ Jesus. (Philippians 4:6–7)

3
Miracle Morning

We were thrilled by Missy's progress. The guidance provided by The Child Study Center proved invaluable to us in more ways than one.

As we witnessed significant milestones in Missy's progress, we grew in our confidence as parents. We continued to make our monthly trips to the center and we basked in the strides Missy was making.

I had finally ceased my worrying about her. She was developing beautifully. Instead, I found myself worrying about another child – a little girl just about Missy's age who was also sight-impaired. She was the daughter of a young man Phil had known in high school when their families were backyard neighbors. Phil hadn't seen him in years.

Mutual friends constantly encouraged us to contact the couple. However, since we didn't know them well and we had no idea how well they had adjusted to having a special child, we simply didn't know how to approach them. True enough, we did have a common bond – as everyone had said – however, we felt awkward about initiating the contact. Our hesitancy caused weeks to creep into months as we continued to postpone calling them.

Little did we know, they were hearing about us as often as we were hearing about them. Friends and acquaintances of theirs repeatedly suggested they call us. However, they were just as hesitant as we were — and all for the same reasons! Almost two years later, we still had not made contact with one another.

Then our miracle morning came. It began as anything but a miracle. It was, however, a beautiful spring Sunday. Missy and I were dressed in our Sunday best, waiting next to our driveway for Phil to back the car out of the garage.

Suddenly, he got out of the car, closed the garage door and announced, "We can't go."

"What do you mean, we can't go?" I lamented.

Phil looked helpless. "I'm sorry, honey. The car battery is dead. We must have left a door cracked last night."

I looked down at the diaper bag, all packed, complete with warmed bottles, extra diapers and Missy's beloved stuffed clown. "I've got an idea," I said. "Let's walk to church!"

Phil looked startled. "You've got to be kidding. It's ten miles to our church!"

"No, I mean let's walk to the church down the street from here. It's only two or three blocks, and besides I've been wanting to visit there."

"Well, okay," Phil said reluctantly as he glanced at his watch. "But let's hurry. If there's two things I can't stand, one's being late for church, and the other is having to sit up in the very front. And if we're late I just know we'll have to sit up front!"

Down the street we went. We must have been quite a sight, Missy's blonde head bobbing as Phil carried her. I was rushing alongside him, toting my purse, Bibles and diaper bag.

When we arrived at our destination, the parking lot of Southern Hills Baptist Church was packed. I uttered a short prayer under my breath for available seats as we stepped inside the double doors of the red brick building. The lobby was empty, with the exception of one deacon who introduced himself as Delmar. He welcomed us warmly and assisted us in getting Missy settled in the nursery. He then showed us to the sanctuary doors, handed us a bulletin and motioned for us to go right in.

Inside, I searched for empty seats and couldn't spot a single one. I winced as I noticed how far it was to the front of the sanctuary. I was thinking that perhaps we could slip out when suddenly an usher spotted us, smiled broadly and motioned us forward. I took one look at him and knew he was already too far forward to suit Phil. Nevertheless, we followed the usher's beckoning. I could feel heat rising in my face as we drew nearer to the front. It seemed he would never stop.

And he didn't — that is, until he reached the second row from the front of the sanctuary. There, the man finally ushered us into the last two seats available! Two seats which *just happened* to be right next to the parents of the visually impaired child we had heard about for over a year and a half.

After this initial meeting that went beyond coincidence, we became close friends with the couple, Pat and Sheryl, and fell in love with their beautiful little girl, Sharmon. She had a motor disorder in addition to her visual impairment. We couldn't wait to tell them about the program we had discovered in Oklahoma City.

They were ecstatic to learn of the center and soon our two families were making the trips to the city together. As time went by, that unforgettable Sunday morning slipped farther into the past, but the miracle of it all has never left our hearts.

We later learned that the church had been so packed on the morning we met, that the ushers had been forced to open the side partitions of the sanctuary to allow for extra seating. Even then, every seat had been taken. But shortly before the service began, a couple, who previously had occupied the two front seats we took, had been tapped on the shoulder by a nursery worker.

The worker had explained that the nursery department was short-handed that morning and had asked if the man and his wife would mind helping. The two agreed to assist in the nursery and, therefore, they had vacated the two seats next to our friends immediately prior to our arrival. Moments later, Phil and I were able to be seated there. As far as the young couple knew, they had simply agreed to volunteer in the nursery — a simple act of service. Little do they know to this day, they were actually setting the stage for a miracle — the first of many! Regrettably, we never learned their names.

The steps of good men are directed by the Lord. He delights in each step they take. (Psalms 37:23)

4

What Next, Lord?

Our trips to Oklahoma City gave Sheryl and me a perfect opportunity to get to know each other. We chattered incessantly about the many things which were of interest to young mothers, particularly with regard to the common bond we shared.

We devoted hours of conversation to our daughters and their needs. Since our first meeting, we had wondered if there were other parents of special children in Tulsa. Surely they were struggling with feelings of frustration and helplessness just like we experienced. If only we could find them, perhaps we could start a support group, we reasoned, but we both realized that this idea was a big "if."

Then something rather amazing happened. On one of our monthly trips to Oklahoma City, we arrived in the city early. We decided to use the extra time doing what all young mothers love to do — shopping for baby clothes. I drove our car to a gas station and asked for directions to the nearest shopping center. Obviously in a hurry, and showing little interest in our quest, the attendant rattled off some rather hazy directions to us.

After following his directions, two intersections and a left-hand turn later, we were relieved to see a small strip of shops.

We headed down the length of the strip, passing a paint store, a shoe store, and a fabric shop, but no baby clothes shop. We continued studying each store until we reached the end of the L-shaped strip.

Looking straight ahead, we were intrigued with what we saw. There, in front of our car, was a huge sign: "Oklahoma Library for the Blind." Neither of us had known that such a place existed, much less where it was located. Excitedly, we pulled into the parking space that seemed to be awaiting our arrival.

Inside, a pretty brunette greeted us, asking how she might assist us. We told her about Missy's and Sharmon's visual impairments, and that we were seeking resources to help our daughters in their development. She asked us where we were from. When we mentioned Tulsa, she looked surprised and enthusiastically exclaimed there was someone who would very much like to meet us. In a second, she was heading toward the back of the library, which was lined with enormous steel bookshelves and the largest books I had ever seen.

Moments later, a middle-aged lady with salt-and-pepper hair rushed from the back to greet us. She spoke so fast, we could hardly keep up with what she was saying.

From her, we learned, however, that the library could provide us with invaluable materials for our little girls – completely free of charge. Later, they would even supply "talking book machines" and children's "talking books" for the blind.

But the peak of her enthusiasm focused on *us.* She was thrilled to be in contact with parents of visually limited children from the Tulsa area.

"How did you happen to find us?" she asked. "We've been wanting to establish a direct contact with Tulsa. You see, we have a list of parents of visually impaired children in Tulsa, but we need someone who will be willing to serve as a liaison between this library and the parents. Would you be willing to help us?"

We gladly agreed. It seemed incredible to us. Here was the very resource we had been looking for – the person who could put us in contact with other families of visually impaired children in our city. We could never have found her on our own, but God knew exactly where she was and He led us directly to her.

After making some initial plans through which we could provide assistance for each other, we realized we were overdue for our appointment at The Child Study Center. Quickly bidding the ladies goodbye, we rushed to our car.

As I hurriedly closed the car door, I commented to Sheryl, "You know, it's getting exciting just putting the key in the ignition. There's no telling where God will take us next!"

Little did we know!

You chart the path ahead of me, and tell me where to stop and rest. Every moment, you know where I am. You know what I am going to say before I even say it. You both precede and follow me, and place your hand of blessing on my head. (Psalms 139:3-5)

5

But God Can!

It was our third trip to Oklahoma City together. All the way to the center, Sheryl and I shared the hopes we held for our children. We weren't at all prepared for the disturbing news Sheryl received from the professionals that day.

With as much sensitivity as possible, they explained that Sharmon was significantly developmentally delayed and required more therapy than they could offer long distance, on a monthly basis. Sharmon needed professional attention and therapy on a daily basis. Because of Pat's job, it was out of the question for her family to move to Oklahoma City. And there were still no services available for children like Missy and Sharmon in the Tulsa area.

A cloud of discouragement hung heavy in our hearts as we returned home. The outlook for Sharmon was not good if she didn't receive the professional attention she needed early in her life.

Then, parting the clouds of doubt, God reached down into our hearts and planted an idea. His thought seemed to fall on us simultaneously. We began to talk about how wonderful it would be if there could be a center in Tulsa like the one in Oklahoma City. And why couldn't there be? Surely there was a hospital or school in Tulsa that would be willing to start up such a program.

The more we talked about the prospect of the new center for Tulsa, the more our excitement mounted. God seemed to be kindling a fire of desire in our hearts. By the time we reached our homes, we had already formulated our plan of action. The next week we set up appointments with administrators of medical and educational facilities in Tulsa. As we shared our vision with these professionals, time and again we received the same disheartening response, only in different forms.

"Come back in a year or so. Perhaps then we can help you. Right now, we just don't have the funds," one said. Another explained they didn't have adequate staff. Another complained of inadequate space for their existing programs and expressed the unlikelihood of establishing new ones.

After weeks of searching, I was ready to give up. But Sheryl remained undaunted. I had come to recognize a precious quality in her. She had a kind of faith that is rare to behold. I was captivated by her prayerful perseverance. She managed to talk me into going with her to consult with one last pediatrician.

Meeting with hospital directors and administrators was not an easy task for Sheryl or me. Neither of us was experienced in presenting proposals to professionals – much less medical and educational professionals. Then too, of course we had no choice but to take Missy and Sharmon along, and they needed constant attention as most toddlers do. To make matters worse, this last doctor seemed especially formidable, as he sat behind his large wooden desk. "And what can I do for you ladies?" he asked with a somber face.

"It's about our little girls," I explained. "You see, they're visually impaired and they need a special school that will help them develop to their full potential. And there is no school like that in Tulsa."

Sheryl continued on, explaining to him about the program in Oklahoma City and the lack of services in our home area.

"We know of other children who need these services. Surely you know of a center or hospital that could develop such a program. So far no one has been willing or able to do so." She talked on and on. When she ran out of points to cover, I picked up where she left off.

When we both ran out of points, the doctor sat back in his chair and thought for a while. The silence in his office was deafening and it seemed endless to Sheryl and me. Finally, he laid down his pencil, studied us for a moment, and said, "Ladies, if you want this school, you'll just have to start it yourselves."

We were both dumbfounded. That was undoubtedly the most preposterous statement we had ever heard! I was outraged by his response. I managed, however, to keep my cool until we stepped right outside his office.

But the minute the door was closed, I began expressing my feelings. "I can't believe he would say such a thing to us! He's bound to know there's no way we could even *think* of doing anything like that. I mean, after all, he knows how much is involved – he's a doctor!"

We walked through the heavy doors of the medical center. I was still angrily rattling on as we settled the girls into the car. In fact, quite some time had passed, and I was still expressing my sentiments about the whole affair when it dawned on me — Sheryl hadn't said a word since we left the doctor's office! Her face registered a surprising blend of peace and confidence.

Then the thought hit me! "Sheryl! You're *not* thinking what I think you're thinking, are you?"

Sheryl smiled sweetly.

"Sheryl! We wouldn't know where to begin to establish a school like that!"

Sheryl's face lit up as she finally spoke, "But God knows."

I suddenly felt a knot forming in my stomach. "Oh, Sheryl, I know that's true, but if all these doctors think it would be so expensive, I don't even want to know how expensive it would be! And, Sheryl, we can't raise the kind of funds we'd need for a project like this."

"But God can," she said softly. "And if we'll just trust Him, He'll help us. I know He will!" Her soothing voice calmed my spirit.

I sat quietly for a moment or two, pondering her words. Then I realized, for the first time in my life, I was face-to-face with a serious question. Did I really believe God could do *anything* — move any mountain? As a child in Sunday school I had memorized Scriptures about it. All my life, I had sung hymns about it, but now I needed to know if I *really* believed it.

It was easier to believe God could supply the money for the school than to believe He could use

Sheryl and me to start it. We knew so little — so little about finances, administration, special education, staffing — and all the rest that one would need to know in order to start a program like the one we envisioned.

But Sheryl's convictions stirred something in me. She seemed to have enough faith for the two of us.

I thought about it all the way home, and by the time I reached my house, I found myself remembering the faith that I had embraced as a small child and believing that maybe — just maybe — with God's help, our mountain *could* be moved.

And so, with great fear and trembling, I took Sheryl's strong hand of faith, and together we stepped out and believed God for a twentieth-century miracle — a school for blind and partially sighted children, in our own home city — Tulsa, Oklahoma.

> For if you had faith even as small as a tiny mustard seed you could say to this mountain, 'Move!' and it would go far away. Nothing would be impossible. (Matthew 17:20)

6
A Dream Embraced

I could hardly wait to share our exciting plans with Phil. When I walked through the front door that evening, he was sitting in his favorite brown-velveteen, easy chair, reading the newspaper.

"Well, honey, guess what Sheryl and I are going to do," I spoke. His paper moved ever so slightly. "What's that, hon?"

"Start a school for visually impaired children," I proudly announced. "It's going to be wonderful – complete with special teachers, therapists and medical consultants."

Phil slowly lowered his paper, exposing a stunned expression. "You've got to be kidding! But you don't know the first thing about how to start a program like that!"

I smiled, remembering what Sheryl had said. "You're right, but God does!" came my confident, though somewhat-plagiarized reply.

Phil gazed at me, his face registering even more concern. "But, Marcia, we don't have the money to start a program like that."

I rushed on excitedly. "I know we don't, but God does! And Sheryl says, if we'll just trust Him, He'll meet our needs." I sat down on the ottoman next to him.

"Sweetheart," I continued, "the need for this center is great. All the doctors and other professionals we've met admit that. Yet, they can't help us. We have no one else to depend on. And you're right — we obviously can't depend on ourselves. We don't have the knowledge we need to undertake an endeavor like this. We've just got to trust God to lead us."

Phil sighed. The paper now lay folded in his lap. His eyes were filled with concern. "Marcia, do you have any idea how much money you would need for this kind of special school?"

The question was sobering. The answer, even more so. I didn't have a hint of an idea. "No, I guess I don't," I responded. "And Sheryl has her heart set on opening the school this fall."

Phil straightened in his chair. "You mean *this* fall?"

I nodded. It did sound outlandish and unrealistic. But then, we *were* asking God for a *miracle.*

The next day, though I was busy with personal errands, I wasn't thinking about the broken toaster that needed to be fixed or the grocery shopping I had to do. My mind kept replaying the concerns Phil had expressed the evening before. We had no money to begin the project and no idea of where to start. Was this idea simply wishful thinking on our part?

For a week or two, we received no direction. Then one evening I was invited to a gathering of the wives of members of The Brookside Lions Club of Tulsa. The women were discussing the reorganization of the wives' auxiliary. Phil was a Brookside Lions Club member, and I had been invited to assist in getting the group started once again.

As we sat drinking punch in the living room of the home of one of the wives, we discussed the pros and cons of activating the group. After a short discussion, one lady spoke up as the whole group gave full attention to her. "Well, I'd like to see this group reorganize. But if we do, I don't want to just sit around and sip punch all day. I want to get involved in a worthwhile project – one that will make a difference. One we can really sink our teeth into!"

Her words were almost too good to be true. Sheryl and I certainly had such a project. As I listened my mind raced – do I dare present it to them? Here? Now? Before I had time to lose my nerve, I spoke up.

"Excuse me. I think I know of such a project. Would you be interested in hearing about it?" Suddenly, I had the floor.

The ladies listened with heartfelt concern. And when I left that evening, twelve other ladies began to share our dream. Within days of our decision to believe God for a miracle, a group of women committed themselves to band together and undergird Sheryl and me in our efforts, by raising funds for the opening of our needed school.

Once again, God had divinely intervened and was paving the way with each step we took! He had honored our prayers.

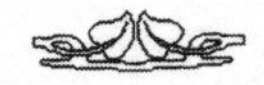

I am the Lord, the God of all mankind; is there anything too hard for me? (Jeremiah 32:27)

7

Rainbow Dreams, Miracle Realities

It was the spring of 1972, and now that the Brookside Lions Club Auxiliary of Tulsa had officially reorganized, their first project was to raise the necessary funds to open the doors of Tulsa's first preschool for visually impaired children and infants. Deciding on a fund-raising project was the first order of business.

A garage sale was the first idea presented. I thought it was a splendid suggestion. I had never been part of a garage sale, and although I couldn't imagine people coming to buy other people's discarded belongings, it all sounded easy enough. We chose a date and the plans were set in motion.

A short time later, we began to prepare for the sale. Old plastic containers, broken cameras, semi-worn furniture and used vases lined the driveway of a willing Lions Club Auxiliary member. Never before had I seen such a vast array of junk. I was exuberant to think of the funds we would raise. This project represented the first step in our faith journey.

The weekend of the big event proved to be dreary and damp. However, the rainy weather didn't deter our customers. The hours passed quickly, and soon the last of the items had been carted off by a junk dealer.

I couldn't wait to get home to report the results. Phil was already there when I arrived home that evening. I burst through the door, feeling a great sense of accomplishment and exclaimed, "Well, honey, guess how much we made."

"How much?" he asked, with an expectant tone.

"Sixty-five dollars," I stated with pride.

Now, Phil was never a person given to excess worry, but suddenly I saw signs of genuine anxiety on his face. He shook his head in disbelief. "Sixty-five dollars!" The unfamiliar worry lines made even deeper creases in his brow. "Honey, do you realize what it's going to take just to get the school's doors open – that's assuming you've got doors to open – which you don't."

I shook my head.

"You'll need at least 2,000 to 3,000 dollars to start a school like the one you're envisioning."

There were a few moments of silence as I winced at the truth of his statement. "I suppose you're right. I just don't know what else we can do at this point."

For the next twenty-four hours, my mind was consumed with questions about how we could raise the needed funds. Finally, I confronted God with our dilemma. "Lord, we've done all we know to do. You'll have to tell us where to go from here. I have no idea how to raise the kind of funds we'll need. Why, I haven't seen a fund-raiser bring in that kind of money since. . . . "

Suddenly the thoughts were coming to me in a rush. When I taught speech at one of the local high schools, it was my responsibility to direct the freshman class play each year. I chose a children's theater play, "The Wizard of Oz," as my last production. I was privileged to work with exceptionally talented and dedicated students. Through that venture alone, we raised over $1,300 for their class. Perhaps this was our answer!

I wondered, would it be possible to produce the play once again? I knew I could direct it again, but it had been two years since I had even had contact with my former students. Would they be willing to give sacrificially of their summer days to put the production on again? Would they, too, be willing to dream our dream? "Lord," I prayed, "are these thoughts from you?"

Sheryl was thrilled with the idea! However, the more excited she became, the more I realized what a large project we were considering. That's when my sense of panic set in. When Sheryl made up her mind and believed something was in God's will, there was simply no turning back. "It's perfect," she proclaimed.

"But, Sheryl, I haven't even seen my students in so long. What if they've moved away, or have jobs, or —"

Sheryl broke in. "Marcia, just start contacting them. You'll see, God can meet this need as well."

So, I started calling. I began with my Tinman. "Hello, Randy — this is Mrs. Mitchell. Do you remember me?" One by one, I contacted the students who had played each character. Dorothy, the Scarecrow, the Cowardly Lion, and the list continued. Each and every one was more than excited over the idea. Those whose schedules would not permit them to participate gave me names of other young people who might help. In a few days we had a full cast!

But there was also the matter of set design, ticket sales, publicity, sound, lights and a host of other components which make up an effective live theater production. To add to our worries, we had no auditorium, and no funds for rental — that is, except for the $65 we had raised from the garage sale. That amount could get us started, but would hardly be enough to cover our production costs. Perhaps, I thought, the Lions Club Auxiliary would be willing to help. I was right. They were more than enthusiastic about the idea.

I presented to them the problem of cost for the project. The original production had operated on a budget of $500. And with that production, we didn't have the problem of locating or renting an auditorium since it had been held in the school.

The auxiliary members thought they had the perfect solution. They suggested I present the need to the Brookside Lions Club Board. The wives felt that since the club had the funds, they would be more than happy to provide the $500, if I would simply present the project and the need to them.

"But you don't understand," I protested. "I wouldn't do well talking to a group of men, especially when it involves asking for money. I'd get nervous and talk too fast."

The women only smiled, patted me on the back and said, "Oh, of course you can. We'll make all the arrangements."

I could feel my legs trembling as my clammy hand knocked on the front door where the Brookside Lions Club Board meeting was being conducted. Inside, I was received with polite smiles and nods. Finally, they came to the appointed time of the agenda for me to present our need for funds.

I showed a slide presentation of the previous production of "The Wizard" and followed with a talk about the needs of visually impaired children.

As I raced on through my speech, my voice began to tremble. I talked on and on. The longer I talked, the more my voice trembled and so I talked even faster, until finally one man raised his hand. "Yes, sir?" I asked softly.

Plainly and deliberately in a deep voice, he asked, "What is it you want?"

Silence filled the room. I swallowed hard. "Sir, we need $500."

Brusquely, though not unkindly, he said, "I move we write her a check and let her go home." And that is precisely what they did!

I never knew which God used more that evening, my nervousness and long-winded tendency, or their big hearts, but it was obvious to me God was at work.

We had the needed funds and a cast. Young people from all over the Tulsa area gathered once again to create the musical fantasy. Most of the students had their old costumes or knew where they could be found.

Plans were made for alterations or for the purchase of new costumes, and before long, sounds of singing Munchkins could be heard throughout our neighborhood as we worked feverishly in our backyard to pull the show together.

Somehow, word of our efforts spread. The students helped arrange for professional lighting and sound equipment. A recreation center for the disabled offered the use of their auditorium free of charge.

All aspects of the production seemed to be falling into place, with one exception. When directing the play two years before, the school had a stage manager/technical director on staff. He took on the entire responsibility for the technical design of the set for my production. I attempted to call to see if he, too, might help, but unfortunately he'd moved out of state!

In my college days, I always avoided set design and construction. My drama coach constantly admonished me that someday I'd be sorry. Well, that day had come. Once again, I became acutely aware of my need for divine assistance. Once again, God proved faithful.

A friend who had worked on sets for other local productions offered his time and talents. Still, he needed more technical information from me than I was able to give. I desperately longed for even part of the crew who had so masterfully constructed my original set. We did, however, begin work on several of the simpler parts of the set. I could only pray about the rest.

A critical need arose for a particular kind of paint for some of the scenery. I scoured Tulsa in search of it. Finally, after a day-long search, I checked at one last store. Inside, a handsome young man walked over to offer his assistance. As I turned to speak, he looked at me with astonishment. "Mrs. Mitchell! I can't believe it's you. Do you remember me?"

I hated to admit that I didn't, so I stalled with a hesitant response.

He broke into a wide smile. "I understand how you might not. It's been a couple of years. I'm T.A. I was the assistant to the technical director who built the sets for your freshman class production of 'The Wizard of Oz.' You know, I've really missed that kind of work. I'd like to do it again someday."

My jaw dropped. I could hardly believe what I was hearing. What would the chances have been of my finding this young man on my own? I hadn't even known the names of those who had served on that stage crew, much less the name of the technical assistant. But God knew. I was astounded at His ability to orchestrate events as He moved us into position to receive His divine provision.

By the next evening, T.A. was there to answer the myriad of questions about the set that I had been unable to address. He put his talents to work and created a host of outstanding technical effects.

The Lions Club Auxiliary devoted themselves untiringly to ticket sales and publicity. And the media was extraordinarily supportive. Interestingly, the best coverage we received was unsolicited – at least unsolicited by any of us. God, on the other hand, seemed to be working overtime in that area.

Bill Donaldson, an entertainment editor with "The Tulsa Tribune," wrote:

> "The Wizard of Oz" has no monopoly on making dreams come true. For many Tulsans are working to be sure that a special dream comes true for blind and partially sighted children in the community.

He was right! But what a lot of folks may not have realized was, there was a Source far greater than any storybook wizard who was making our dream come true — a Source who *creates* the rainbows and the dreams! And it was He who was transforming them into a reality!

Following a successful five-day run, we closed the show on August 27, 1972, with $2,700 in a special account for our new school.

Long after the last performance was over, Dorothy's song of rainbows, skies of blue and dreams coming true was still ringing in my heart.

Yes, when God gives birth to those dreams — they really do come true!

> Now glory be to God who by his mighty power at work within us is able to do far more than we would ever dare to ask or even dream of — infinitely beyond our highest prayers, desires, thoughts, or hopes. (Ephesians 3:20)

8
The Little White Schoolhouse

Despite the countless times we witnessed God's miraculous provision, each new experience was no less amazing than the one before. God was always one step ahead of us. Our first school site was a classic example of His leading.

During one of the final performances of "The Wizard," I was standing at the back of the darkened auditorium watching as colorful Munchkins danced and sang in high-pitched voices when my focus on the talented young performers was diverted by a voice beside me.

"It's a great show!" a man said. "The children love it!" The enthusiastic voice belonged to a young man who served on the staff at the Recreation Center for the Physically Limited where the play was being produced.

I thanked him for his kindness and once again was caught up in the production when he whispered, "Where is your new school going to be located?"

Hesitantly I responded, "I'm not sure. We've looked into spaces at churches, and we've approached a few schools, but so far, nothing seems to be working out."

"But I just saw in the paper where you're planning to open the school in just a few weeks!" he replied.

"We are!" I said. "We just don't know where as yet."

A wave of disbelief swept across his face. Leaning forward, trying to keep his voice low, he looked at me directly. "You mean you're planning to open this school a few weeks from now, but you don't know where?"

Trying not to sound too nonchalant about it, nor too overly concerned, I said, "That's right." (God hadn't revealed that part to us yet.)

He scratched his head. "Tell me, what kind of a location are you looking for?"

Quickly I responded, "Ideally, we'd like a little house we can fix up. The problem is, we can't pay much in the way of rent." I went on to elaborate on the number of rooms and other specifics we desired for the school.

"You know," he said, "this center has a place that might be perfect for you. They're just using it for storage right now. But maybe, just maybe, they'd be willing to let you use it on a rent-free basis for a year or so. It might be worth a try. How about coming over to see it tomorrow?" I told him I'd be there.

The following morning, we met at the location which was next door to the center where the play was being presented. There, a small, white, frame house was almost hidden from view by a jungle of weeds and overgrown shrubs. I had never noticed it before. Both entrances were barely accessible due to the overgrowth. Still, it looked enticing and God somehow gave us the vision to imagine what it could become.

Inside were four small rooms, a kitchen, a full bath and a front entrance area. There was a sink in one of the rooms, set at just the right height for a child.

Later we learned a doctor had owned the house years before and he had had the sink installed. Why he had it placed so low was a mystery to us, but we knew it was perfect for our needs. Though the walls and floors were in tremendous disrepair, I could see that with a little paint, a lot of elbow grease and some tender loving care, it would be just right!

The center's young staff member was as thrilled as I was. He assured me he would make every effort to arrange for us to be able to use the little house. He did exactly that. Within the week, it was offered to us on a rent-free basis for as long as we could use it.

At last we had our "schoolhouse." We were overjoyed. But we were equally overwhelmed with the monumental task of renovating it.

Through the last searing days of an Oklahoma August we worked and we dreamed. We chopped brush, pulled weeds, mowed, patched walls, scrubbed floors, painted walls, repaired windows and scoured every inch of the small house.

We stretched the few dollars allotted for renovation as far as our imaginations would allow. When we ran short of funds, and the old, drab floor tiles were still begging to be covered, we gathered donated carpet samples and created a rather delightful and colorful patchwork effect.

The church where we had had our miraculous meeting with Sharmon's family hosted a toy party for us and showered us with dozens of items from our "wish list." When we realized we had nothing to display them on, we rounded up old used shelves from garage and junk sales. Though they were battered by years of wear, we were able to transform them with several coats of brightly colored paint.

By the time we had hung the last curtain, all funds for renovating the house had been depleted. We literally hung the last curtain by threading a shoestring through a curtain and tacking each end with thumbtacks. It remained that way as a reminder of the literal "shoestring budget" we would operate on in order to survive during those early years.

Meanwhile, a local attorney heard about our efforts and offered to assist us with the legal paperwork involved in establishing a non-profit organization. (And non-profit we certainly were!)

During one of the quieter moments of those hectic summer days, Sheryl and I were sitting at my dining room table, fine tuning some plans for the school. Papers were strewn before us, and we were in deep discussion when the phone rang. It was the attorney. He asked for the name of our school.

We were both caught off-guard. We had been so busy getting ready to open our new school, we hadn't given a thought to a name! The attorney was insistent. He needed a name before he could progress further.

We knew of The Lighthouse Centers for the Blind in Houston and New York. We, too, would be serving blind people – except ours would be "little ones." Perhaps The Lighthouse would allow us to use the same name, if we would modify ours to read – The Little Light House!

Within a few days, we received their blessings and officially settled on the name, The Little Light House, along with the motto, "Lighting the way for little ones."

We removed the old plywood from the original sign that stood in front of the little house, and hand-painted over it in bright red letters: "The Little Light House." The lettering was amateurish, but cost-effective and neat enough.

By early fall, our little white schoolhouse was almost ready to open. God was meeting our every need.

Trusting means looking forward to getting something we don't yet have — for a man who already has something doesn't need to hope and trust that he will get it. But if we must keep trusting God for something that hasn't happened yet, it teaches us to wait patiently and confidently. (Romans 8:24-25)

9
Kristi's Calling

Earlier that summer, while I was focusing on the musical theater production, Sheryl was searching for a teacher. Neither of us knew the first thing about recruiting or hiring, and we knew even less about locating a teacher with the educational credentials *and* the heart needed for a school like ours. All we could do was pray and petition for God's provision.

We decided to consult one of our local universities. Although they didn't offer training that specializes in the education of the visually impaired, we thought they might provide names of promising teacher candidates. It was a productive decision. The contact led to a young woman who was nearing graduation. She was highly recommended to us. Sheryl gave her a call, and an appointment was scheduled.

In a typical job interview, the location of the workplace would be discussed. The pay schedule would be reviewed. The job description would be presented, and the challenges and benefits of the job and the conditions of the work setting would be covered.

When Kristi arrived for her interview, Sheryl was peacefully oblivious to all of that as well as the marked contrast between what we were offering Kristi and that which she would be offered in practically any other school to which she might apply.

Instead, Sheryl enthusiastically shared about our efforts to open the new school. She told Kristi about the play that was being produced in order to raise enough funds to move ahead. She explained about the program in Oklahoma City and their offer to assist in our efforts to locate other families in need of services.

At that time, she wasn't able to tell Kristi the location or the name of the center, or how much she would be paid or even if she would be paid. She couldn't tell her how many pupils she would eventually have.

We obviously had no benefits to offer her, no vacation plan, no guidelines, no previously established curriculum, no equipment, no tests, no forms. We had only dreams and visions, hope and faith.

Nevertheless, Kristi accepted the position. She heard all that was important to her. She heard God calling her to teach the little ones who would come to The Little Light House. And she responded in simple, child-like obedience to the voice of her heavenly Father. As a result, our new school had a teacher!

God blesses those who obey him; happy the man who puts his trust in the Lord. (Proverbs 16:20)

10
Colors That Smell and Bumps That Spell

The challenge that lay before Kristi was enough to intimidate the most experienced of teachers. She was acutely aware of her own inadequacies. Her course work at the local university hadn't prepared her to teach the visually handicapped, and her student teaching had not given her the amount of experience she needed to establish a new curriculum. Nonetheless, she knew God had called her to the task, but she also realized she was going to need divine assistance, so she called a close friend to pray with her every morning at 5:30.

Soon after Kristi accepted the position, parents began hearing of our efforts to start a new school and contacted us to make arrangements for enrolling their children. Upon interviewing them, Kristi realized that every child was functioning on a different level in almost every developmental area. Consequently, each had an individual set of special needs, and some had other disabling conditions as well.

One handsome, five-year-old boy had been born with a hydrocephalic condition. He was blind, was unable to crawl or walk and could barely sit up by himself.

Sharmon was two years old, visually impaired and significantly developmentally delayed due to her motor disorder. Missy, on the other hand, was visually impaired, but functioning at a normal developmental level. Brian was a bright, two-and-a-half-year-old toddler who was totally blind from birth. And there was the pretty little brunette, four years of age, who was totally blind with no language skills and she had been diagnosed with autistic tendencies.

Kristi tirelessly devoted herself to reading anything that would provide information which would enable her to design a prescriptive program for each child.

The Child Study Center in Oklahoma City provided counsel for her. Dr. Richard Mills, a kind-hearted ophthalmologist, and Dr. Wes Little, a caring university professor, also offered to assist her. Each offered excellent insights into how to plan for the diverse needs of the children.

Obviously the ideal class structure would be one which enabled each child to benefit from every moment spent at The Little Light House. And yet the diversification of developmental levels and needs required a different set of learning activities and exercises for each child.

Unfortunately, there were no comparable programs in our area that modeled how this could be done. Finally, Kristi concluded, the only way the ideal could be attained was with the help of volunteers.

We issued an appeal to the community. Before long, five dedicated ladies responded to our plea. They came willingly and with their whole hearts!

Kristi trained each one to carry out the personalized programs prescribed for each child. She developed an intriguing "activity card" system that enabled her to change each child's activities on a daily or as-needed basis.

Hours of preparation were involved for each child, and yet we never heard Kristi complain. I was amazed at her boundless energy, her positive spirit and her seemingly inexhaustible reservoir of ideas.

Finally, the day for which we had all been so eagerly preparing arrived. It was October 3, 1972 – a day to remember!

Lovely autumn weather greeted us. Missy and Sharmon arrived early with Sheryl and me for their first day of school. Later our volunteers arrived – first Delores, then Nancy, Margaret, and Ruth. When the last one arrived, we all gathered in the back room to pray.

Soon after, the three other preschoolers joined Missy and Sharmon. Clinging tightly to the hands of their mothers, they toddled or were carried into the little schoolhouse.

The moms were as excited as the children. At last, they had a place where their children could receive the specialized training and stimulation they needed.

The volunteers and Kristi gathered in one of the classrooms to start the day as moms watched through one-way, glass observation windows. Kristi led the volunteers as voices melodiously rang out –

Good morning to you, to each one of you.
We're all in our places with smiles on our faces,
now this is the way we start a new day!

A short time later, each volunteer paired up with the child to whom they were assigned and began working on their individual activities. Missy and her volunteer giggled with delight as they took turns blowing a Ping-Pong ball back and forth across the table. Little did Missy realize the fun she was having was a visual exercise to better enable her to track moving objects with her eyes.

Brian busily colored on large sheets of paper as his volunteer watched and lavished him with "oohs" and "ahs" of encouragement. Though his eyes couldn't see the colors, the grape-scented purple marker and the lemon-scented yellow one enabled him to distinguish one from the other, all the while sharpening his sense of smell.

Later, his fingers searched for bumps on sheets of paper, an exercise that would prepare him to eventually read "bumps" that would spell words in braille.

Another child's volunteer was receiving instruction from Kristi in implementing exercises that his therapist had recommended for him.

Sharmon was astride a toy pony. Her volunteer softly coaxed her to use her feet to make the pony move. This activity could eventually help Sharmon to crawl and then to walk.

Another little girl was being softly persuaded by her volunteer to put her hand in a pan of lukewarm water to help her overcome her fear of water.

(Months later we heard a loud splash and then waves of laughter. The same child who had once had such a phobia of water had finally made the plunge into a whole bathtubful of water and straightaway pulled the volunteer right in with her — clothes and all!)

I was amazed and intrigued with the program Kristi had designed. Her ingenious card system was incredibly effective, and within weeks we were observing amazing milestones and unexpected accomplishments in the children.

Our little "dream" school was up and running and in the months to come the program became known as a model program. Kristi had given birth to a "one-on-one" approach to special education for The Little Light House.

Perhaps her success rested in her Source of higher learning. For it was a Source far greater than the course work she had taken at the university. Hers was a divine Source.

> In him lie hidden all the mighty, untapped treasures of wisdom and knowledge. . . . And now just as you trusted Christ to save you, trust him, too, for each day's problems; live in vital union with him. (Colossians 2:3 and 6)

11
Appointed, Anointed and Equipped

As the days turned into weeks, the business affairs of The Little Light House began to mount. The mail brought donations, bills and professional correspondence — all of which required a response. It became increasingly evident that the day-to-day operation of the center would require the services of a full-time executive director.

We were paying Kristi only $200 a month, yet even that slight sum stretched the limits of our faith. We knew we couldn't possibly afford to pay a professional administrator.

There was only one solution. Sheryl or I would have to assume these responsibilities until we could afford to hire a director with the needed experience and skills. It was around this time that we learned Sheryl was pregnant with her second child. Consequently, she couldn't take on the workload involved in the director's position. So I assumed the role of interim director at a token fee until a professional could be hired. Though Sheryl and I remain friends to this day, the demands of her rapidly growing family didn't allow her to remain as directly involved as we both might have desired. Still, the effect of *her* strong faith enabled me to continue on.

However, I felt totally unequipped for my newly assumed position. My only comfort was in the fact that it would only be for a limited time. We hoped the center would soon be financially stable and I could go back to being a housewife and mom.

To keep the workload manageable, the decision was made to restrict class sessions to two days a week for several months. In retrospect, I can't imagine how Kristi and I would have functioned if we had decided otherwise. Within the first nine months of The Little Light House's existence, the pupil population more than tripled and the workload quadrupled!

We were astounded at how much there was to do. Our workdays were long. Most days began at 6:30 AM and rarely ended earlier than 6:30 PM. Sometimes speaking engagements required our presence in the evenings. The demands were exhausting.

When classes weren't in session, Kristi's time was devoted to parent and professional conferences, researching the medical conditions of the children, constructing special teaching aids (most were too costly to purchase commercially), developing individualized programs for the new pupils, locating needed equipment, testing children, documenting pupil progress and finalizing plans for the next day of classes.

My time was spent recruiting volunteers, making my way through the stacks of paperwork, developing forms and procedures, ministering to despairing parents, paying bills, setting up file systems and countless other tasks involved in administration.

We raced to keep up with the ever-increasing enrollment and the myriads of new tasks stacking up from day to day.

Neither of us was prepared for the onslaught of work involved in getting a program of this proportion established. We had not come to this point equipped with the skills necessary to establish a school. We were quite a pair — me, a former junior high speech teacher and Kristi, a twenty-one-year-old, young woman, fresh out of college.

Kristi, however, seemed to take it all in stride. The skills she didn't have when she started, she was able to acquire as we went along. Her enthusiasm never waned, her energy level never slackened, and her dedication far exceeded my comprehension. She obviously wasn't working for the money, yet she worked tirelessly twelve to fourteen hours a day — day after day.

I marveled at her zeal and wondered how she maintained her "peaceful" countenance. I was also mystified by a routine to which she seemed extremely committed.

Every day at noon, after the children had gone and we had completed most of the clean-up and set-up tasks, Kristi would disappear into one of the rooms in the back of the little house for about an hour. One day, my curiosity got the best of me. I knocked softly on the door, and she invited me in. There she sat at one of our small children's tables, surrounded by books and note paper. I asked her what she did in the quiet and privacy of the little room each day.

"I just like to spend the middle of my day with the Lord," she explained. "But what are all the books for?" I wanted to know. Covering the table in front of her was a large notebook, and an array of other books.

"Oh, these? They're the books I use to study my Bible."

I was amazed. As a child, I had asked Jesus into my heart and I had committed my life to serving Him. I had memorized Scriptures so I could put gold stars on a chart in Sunday school. But since that time, my exposure to the Bible had been limited to reading a few verses before turning in each evening. The thought of *studying* the Bible had become foreign to me.

Kristi's enthusiastic spirit made me want to know more. She helped me to see that the Bible is our manual for living. "God equips us for whatever we're facing through study of the Bible," she explained. "Then we need only ask Him, and He will enable us to do whatever He calls us to."

So that's it, I thought to myself. That's where Kristi draws her strength. I had had a relationship with God for years. But suddenly, I realized how much I had been missing.

In this position of interim executive director, I had waded into waters far too deep for me to manage on my own. Perhaps that was because I was trying to make it by myself – depending on God only when I got into serious dilemmas. I guess you could call it "crisis praying." Kristi, on the other hand, was drawing strength and guidance from God on a daily basis.

In time, she taught me even more about what she referred to as "spiritual growth." I learned from her that God doesn't always call the equipped, but He will always equip those He calls.

In time, I saw that throughout biblical history God has repeatedly chosen the least likely candidates to carry out His missions. Moses, a man "slow in speech and tongue," was called to be God's spokesman to lead the people out of Egypt and into the Promised Land. David, a mere, red-cheeked shepherd boy, was raised up by God to slay a Philistine giant.

Others too numerous to mention fill the pages of the Bible. All have a common thread. Their sense of inadequacy prompted them to rely on the Almighty, to appropriate His power and His might. And as they did so, they accomplished great things to the glory of God.

It has become clear to me that it is all right for us to feel inadequate — for in our inadequacy, we are far more likely to depend on God and appropriate His power in our lives. For it's at that point that God can really use us!

I learned much from my young teacher. More than anything, I learned from Kristi that biblical principles which existed thousands of years ago are still true today. She was living proof!

> "I am with you; that is all you need. My power shows up best in weak people." Now I am glad to boast about how weak I am; I am glad to be a living demonstration of Christ's power, instead of showing off my own power and abilities. (2 Corinthians 12:9)

12
Divine Requisitions

Friends from near and far learned of our efforts and many wanted to help. Some sent contributions. Even with their support, however, we could only cover the cost of essential needs.

We daily found ourselves fervently petitioning God to meet our needs. I did ask my friends and relatives to check costs of needed items for us, but the prices of classroom and office supplies were so prohibitive, it would always send us back to prayer: "Lord, we beseech you to meet this need."

Our office consisted of an old wooden desk that had been painted numerous times, an old executive chair and an antiquated typewriter. We desperately needed a file cabinet. Our pastor's wife volunteered to help me with the paperwork, but even with her help, the job was nerve-racking without a file cabinet.

Then, one afternoon, I looked up from my work to see a huge, five-drawer file cabinet barely clearing the front door as it was pushed through by a delivery man. I waited until he, too, was through the door before I spoke.

When the cabinet finally came to a rest, a young fellow peered around it. "Delivery!" he announced. "Sign here, please."

I couldn't believe my eyes. A brand-new file cabinet! I looked at the mounds of paper toppling over on my desk. Still, as tempting as it was to accept it, we hadn't ordered a file cabinet, and we certainly couldn't pay for one!

"Sir, I don't know who's supposed to receive this, but it certainly isn't ours! We didn't order one."

He shifted his weight from one foot to the other. "Ma'am, it says right here it's to be delivered to 1007 South Utica."

By this time, people were needing to get past the huge file cabinet which was blocking the small space in our tiny administrative quarters. "Young man, we didn't order that file cabinet. If you leave it here, you'll likely have to come back and get it later."

"Ma'am, I don't know who ordered it. I don't know *why* I'm delivering it. All I know is that it is to be delivered *here*. It has your address on it, and I'm supposed to leave it!" With that he was gone, leaving me absolutely bewildered!

I knew we hadn't ordered it and yet before me was our much-needed file cabinet! I couldn't recall having mentioned the need to anyone. Later that week, I learned that a lady who had befriended The Little Light House had noticed the need and had taken it upon herself to appeal to a local business association to meet it. They had agreed to provide the much-needed file cabinet.

On a day-by-day basis, God continued to work in dramatic ways! On still another occasion we were in desperate need of smocks for the children. Because our students were visually impaired and some were limited by motor disorders, often at lunchtime more food ended up on their fronts than in their stomachs. Smocks would be the perfect solution.

Kristi, our volunteers and I had continued the practice of praying together in the early hours of the day. We called it "flock time." It was during this time when we prayed for smocks. Still they didn't come.

After some time had passed, we reasoned that if we wanted the smocks, we'd simply have to purchase them with the meager cash we had available. I promised the volunteers on a Thursday that by the following Tuesday I would buy the much-needed smocks.

That weekend, I was running errands with my sister when we passed a clothes shop for children. Jayne Ann loves to shop and she asked me if I had time to run into the attractive shop for just a moment.

"I don't think so," I told her. "I really need to get home."

"Oh, come on," she coaxed. "We'll be only a few minutes."

Remembering the smocks, I consented, thinking I might possibly find some there.

We had only been in the store a few minutes and hadn't exchanged a word with anyone, when a lady walked up to me holding a child's smock. "Mrs. Mitchell, is this the kind of smock you need at The Little Light House?"

I gazed at her in disbelief. The smock was perfect. But how did this lady know who I was, or that I was with The Little Light House? And how did she know we needed smocks? Noting my puzzled expression, she pulled out another smock. "If there's a problem with that one, perhaps this one will do."

I was speechless. I'd never seen this lady before. She continued on. "We also have a catalog from which you may choose. Why don't you scan through it and let me know which kind you want, what sizes, colors and how many of each you'll need?"

I finally found my voice. "Thank you," I said, still in a state of bewilderment, "and could you explain the cost breakdown on these?" I was having difficulty deciphering the wholesale catalog.

"Oh, don't you worry about the prices. We're going to take care of that," she said quickly. "You just pick out the ones you need, and I'll see that you get them. No cost to you."

Finally, I could stand it no longer. "Forgive me, but I don't recall having met you. Should I know you?"

"Oh, no," she said and then she smiled. "I'm sorry. I should have told you. Someone came in months ago pricing smocks for you. At the time I didn't know anything about your school. Later, my civic group chose it as a philanthropy project, and that's when I learned about it. Recently, I saw your picture in the paper and I recognized you. I've wanted to do something for The Little Light House – like the smocks – but it kept slipping my mind, that is, until you came in today! I'm so glad you stopped in."

So was I! Once again, as if by divine requisition, our order had been filled. God was still in the miracle-working business and was supplying *all* our needs "from His riches in glory" – to His glory.

And it is he who will supply all your needs from his riches in glory, because of what Christ Jesus has done for us. Now unto God our Father be glory forever and ever. Amen. (Philippians 4:19-20)

13
God's Blueprints

As our pupil population increased, the space in our little house became less and less adequate. Since the backbone of our program revolved around a one-on-one ratio, each additional pupil meant an additional volunteer as well. By the end of our first summer, nineteen children were listed on our roll.

Including Kristi, the volunteers, parents and pupils, Barbara (our volunteer secretary) and myself, there were sometimes more than thirty people packed in the tiny rooms of the small frame house. It was hard to imagine that only nine months earlier, the small space had appeared to provide all the space we would ever need.

Some of the children were non-ambulatory. Consequently, they had to be carried and they required the use of special wheelchairs and adaptive seating. As the adult volunteers worked with the children, they needed space to spread out.

The space problem became more and more critical. Kristi, innovative teacher that she was, even considered hoisting the small chairs up to the ceiling when not in use, and lowering them down for lunchtime. It was never attempted, but we were that desperate in our overcrowded conditions.

Finally, we determined we could not allow one more child to be enrolled. It was a tough decision to make, especially for two administrative novices. Still, it was obvious we had no alternative. Or so we thought.

It had been a long day. The center was finally spic-and-span and ready for the next day of classes. I was at the front desk which was situated only a few feet from the front door. Though I was concentrating on the work at hand, I noticed the front door when it squeaked open. A tiny boy peeked in. He had carrot-red hair. Freckles covered his cheeks, and resting on his pug nose were the thickest glasses I had ever seen.

"Can I help you?" I asked.

His eyes were wide as he studied the room, as though to determine whether it was safe to proceed.

"Would you like to come in?" I rose and stepped nearer the door. The child pushed the door open and stood motionless. He was holding the hand of a short, stocky lady. She stared straight ahead, her eyes unmoving. Her other hand held tightly to the hand of a tiny, blonde-headed girl whose glasses matched those of the boy.

Again, I asked if I could help. By now all three were inside. The woman looked to be in her thirties. Though she never looked in my direction, she finally spoke in a soft voice, "Yes, please. I was wondering if I could enroll my two children?"

The sight of this family was one that will forever be etched in my mind. I asked her if she'd like to be seated. She began feeling for a chair and finally it registered in my mind that she was blind — totally blind. The small boy gently guided her to a chair next to the wall.

Her request was simple. "I've been blind most of my life," she told me. "My husband is also blind. Both of our children are losing their sight as well. I want them to learn as much as possible before their sight deteriorates. Can you help us, please?"

A lump swelled in my throat. Had Kristi and I really prayed about the decision not to enroll any additional children? It was true we had no more space. It might even border on unsafe to bring another child in.

I looked at the mother who was waiting expectantly for an answer. I didn't know what to tell her. "I'll have to confer with our teacher," I said, "and then I'll get back to you. Our enrollment is full, but, well, we'll see what we can do." After we exchanged the necessary information, they made their way to the door and down the ramp.

Kristi and I decided we just couldn't turn them away. The next weekend, we rounded up clear plastic sheeting, electrical tape and carpet samples — all the supplies we needed to transform the small, screened-in porch at the back of the house into one last classroom. The two tots were enrolled a short time later.

It wasn't long after their enrollment that I noticed Kristi working intently at one of the children's tables. She was laboring over a large piece of butcher paper. Lines of squares and rectangles covered the mass of white.

"What in the world are you doing?" I asked.

Kristi, a bit startled at first, glanced at me, then looked proudly at her work. "I'm designing our next facility!"

I looked at the maze of rooms. "Kristi, you've got to be kidding. We're barely making financial ends meet *here,* and we're not even paying rent – only utilities! How do you think we can afford a facility like that? You've drawn twenty or more rooms on that plan."

"I know!" she proclaimed. "See, this room is for gross motor and physical therapy exercises. This area is for creative play and social interaction. This smaller room is for speech therapy. The big room is for large group times, and all of the little rooms off the big rooms are for one-on-one work with children who have attention-span problems. They'll be free from distractions in those small rooms with only their volunteer."

I couldn't believe what I was seeing or hearing! "Kristi, how do you think we can possibly get into a facility like that? We certainly don't have the funds and, besides, that design is ten times the size of what we have now!"

"But we *need* the additional space! And God knows we need it. And He promises to meet our needs as we serve Him. So, if that's true, He must be planning a new location for us and while He's in the process, I just want to pray for *exactly* what we need!"

I couldn't help being a bit amazed as I walked away shaking my head. She had the same kind of faith Sheryl had demonstrated. I also believed God heard our prayers, but I was still intrigued to think that He would answer such a large request and one with such a long list of specifications.

A few weeks had passed when a well-dressed gentleman paid us a visit. He had silvering hair and was quite distinguished in appearance. He walked with a sense of certainty, as though he had important business to conduct and he wanted to get right to it. His manner was the same. He introduced himself as the administrator of a nearby church.

He explained that he and his wife had been watching television on a previous night when a public service announcement aired about The Little Light House. His wife felt strangely impressed that he was to come by and see what the center was all about.

I thanked him for his interest and invited him to tour the school. I talked to him about the special needs of the children, shared with him about our venture in faith and spent some time presenting our overall program to him. He was nice enough, but he seemed eager to be on his way.

Before he left, however, he turned to say, "This is a fine program, but I have to say it's the most 'rinky-dink' facility I've ever seen!" With that he was gone!

After he left, I reflected on this gentleman who seemed to have a softness beneath his "all-business" veneer. I wondered if we would ever see him again.

The following Saturday morning, Kristi and I each received a call from him. "I have a place I'd like you to see," he spoke in a direct, staccato manner, but I could detect kindness in his voice as well. "Can you meet me there this morning?"

Kristi and I both agreed. He gave us an address and a meeting time.

We were filled with curiosity as we pulled up to the large, beige church building. There was a large sign that read "Immanuel Baptist Church." He was right on time. Kristi and I were led to a side entrance and up three flights of stairs. When we reached the top, we were staring down a long hallway with another long corridor to the right and one to the left. Each hall had several doors opening off of it. We headed to the right.

He opened the first door. Inside the huge room were stacks of children's chairs – hundreds of them. Adjoining the large room were several smaller rooms, each one also storing chairs.

We proceeded down the hallway. Each door revealed the same picture – large rooms, with adjacent smaller rooms – *just like the crude plans Kristi had sketched a few weeks earlier.* Her eyes were growing wider with each door he opened. Finally, we came to the end of the hall. The gentleman turned to us.

Seeing our faces, he smiled. "I think we can offer this space to your ministry, if it would meet your needs. There would be no cost to you, other than utilities. We're using it only for storage. Why don't you present it to your board, think it over and get back to us."

Kristi and I almost floated down the three flights of stairs. It was perfect! God had indeed answered our prayers – and so specifically!

A few months later, The Little Light House moved into the spacious facilities that were so graciously offered to us rent-free! Upon closer inspection, we confirmed that the floor plan of our new home fulfilled all the criteria of Kristi's dream plans! Her prayer had been answered. Even though God had His own set of blueprints, they were almost an exact duplication of Kristi's!

> I will answer them before they even call to me. While they are still talking to me about their needs, I will go ahead and answer their prayers! (Isaiah 65:24)

14
A Lesson in Faith

Perhaps it was because "walking by faith" was new to us that we became so acutely aware of God's grace and provisions early on in the ministry. The children were flourishing in their new school — growing and developing. Phil and I were growing, too. Our milestones were spiritual in nature. Phil remembers well his first lesson in faith. It seemed designed especially for him.

He had always been conservative, cautious and never one to take chances needlessly. He found this "faith walking" business rather unnerving at the very beginning. Still, he couldn't argue with the miraculous developments which had taken place through the early months of the school's history.

His position on The Little Light House Board of Directors kept him painfully aware of the perpetual financial needs of the ministry.

Over a year and a half had passed since The Little Light House had opened its doors. The enrollment numbers continued to rise dramatically. The staff had grown proportionately. Needless to say, the operational costs increased as well. Consequently, the challenge of meeting our never-ending financial obligations seemed increasingly overwhelming. Month after month, the bills and payroll payments drained the bank account, leaving barely enough to keep the account open.

During each month, funds trickled in. Sometimes hours and even minutes before critical financial obligations were to be met, the funds would suddenly appear. Typically they came from sources who were unaware of our impending need.

This recurrent financial scenario had finally taken its toll on Phil. Such thoughts were monopolizing his thoughts one evening as I entered the living room after a long day at the school. He had arrived home only minutes before I did. Rather uncharacteristically, I found him pacing in the living room.

"Hi, honey. Have a bad day?" I asked, as I set Missy down, along with the paraphernalia I was carrying.

He stopped short. "Marcia, I've been thinking."

I braced myself. His tone was serious as he continued, "I don't see how we can keep operating like this. For a year and a half the school has been barely making ends meet. We have *no* source of regular income. We never know where the money is going to come from, or even *if* it's going to come. Under these kinds of circumstances, the center can't possibly survive."

I decided dinner preparations would have to wait awhile. "What's really bothering you?" I asked, expressing my puzzlement. "The finances aren't any different than they've been all along."

After a few moments of silence, he answered, "The school's bills have to be paid — and paid on time. Right now that means we need $1,200 day after tomorrow! Rarely is that much money donated over a period of a week or two, much less a day or two. I don't know what we're going to do."

It was an unusual sight. Phil had never been a worrier. Now, he was pacing and stewing! Of course, I could understand. I, too, worried over the financial concerns. But then, on the other hand, God had repeatedly demonstrated His ability to provide over the previous eighteen months.

This realization comforted my heart, yet my mind still wrestled with the needs of the moment.

Could God provide this large amount in so short a time? The hectic demands of the evening finally took precedent over our worrisome conversation. However, the next afternoon I received my answer. Once again, Phil arrived home first. When I entered the living room, he was standing there grinning a rather sheepish grin.

"Hi, honey. What's up now?" I asked with even more curiosity than the day before.

"You're not going to believe it," he said as he handed me an envelope. "This came in today's mail."

The cover letter was from the Downtown Lions Club of Tulsa. It explained that since our school served the blind and visually impaired — their main charity focus — they wanted to get involved. The letter told of their decision to pledge $200 per month to The Little Light House. Furthermore, it was decided to make their pledge six months retroactive. As a result of those decisions, they had enclosed precisely $1,200!

Phil shook his head in amazement. "I never would have believed it, if I hadn't witnessed it firsthand. God really is providing!" He had experienced a lesson in faith that he would treasure for life!

> [God] will always give you all you need from day to day if you will make the Kingdom of God your primary concern. So don't be afraid, little flock. For it gives your Father great happiness to give you the Kingdom. (Luke 12:31-32)

15
The Donut Miracle

As time went on, our faith continued to be stretched by the finances needed to care for God's special children. During these times, God had ways of lovingly reminding us He was still watching over us in ways which left us amazed and sometimes even amused, but always humbled as we witnessed His tender care for us!

One such incident took place shortly after a dramatic growth spurt in our pupil enrollment and volunteer team. Our volunteers proved to be our most valuable asset. They administered individualized prescriptive programs designed to meet the complex needs of our little ones. We were indebted to these caring and enthusiastic individuals.

Because they gave their love, their hearts and their time so unselfishly, we sought ways of expressing our appreciation to them. One of those expressions was to have fresh donuts and hot coffee awaiting their arrival each morning. This idea was well received and quickly became somewhat of a Little Light House tradition.

However, the cost of the donuts multiplied as we amassed a greater number of volunteers. Then funds ran so short that it became evident that the donuts would have to be eliminated from the budget. The cost had become prohibitive.

Though staff members supported my decision, they could not hide their disappointment. In their eyes, I saw a reflection of my own sentiments. It seemed this small gesture was the least we could do in exchange for the help and hard work donated by our beloved volunteers. Still, I thought, if the Lord wanted us to have donuts, He'd just have to supply them. At the same time, I chided myself for thinking that our Father God should be bothered with such a menial matter.

After the donuts were cut from the budget, our staff saw to it that the volunteers were at least offered graham crackers with their coffee. The crackers certainly didn't compare with the donuts, but they could curb one's appetite if there had been no time for breakfast. And they helped deliver the message of our hearts.

Then one morning as I was leaving for work, the phone rang. A man's hurried voice said, "Sorry to bother you. I don't believe we've met, but my daughter recently visited the school you operate. She is so excited about your program for the children that she's spoken of nothing else for two days."

I politely acknowledged his kind remarks.

"Her enthusiasm is rather contagious," he continued. "I'm wondering if I might get involved in some small way."

"That's very thoughtful of you," I answered.

"I don't even know if you can use what I have to offer," he said. "You see, all I have to give you is donuts. I have a donut shop."

"A donut shop?" my mind began to race.

"Yes," he responded. "I'd like to box about thirty dozen donuts to give you. No charge, of course. They'll just be my contribution. Can you use them?"

Use them? I could hardly contain my joy!

When I arrived at the donut shop, I was greeted warmly by a slightly built, gray-haired gentleman. He smiled broadly at me from the opposite side of a well-stocked bakery counter as I expressed our heart-felt appreciation to him. To this day, only the Lord knows who felt the most blessed that morning as I left his shop.

The staff and volunteers looked on with wonder as I presented our unexpected gift. We marveled over the perfect timing of the man's call. When we still had dozens of donuts left over from the first day, we carefully bagged them to be frozen for future use.

Donuts – such a trivial need. And yet, not only did we receive them, we received them in all flavors, kinds and sizes! Anyone who thought God had no time for the minute details of our lives needed to see our freezer!

Two days later, my assistant appeared at my office door. Her eyes were wide with excitement. It seemed that Don, our "donut angel," had called again.

"Marcia," she announced, "more donuts are on the way. Thirty dozen to be exact!"

Within a few days, our new friend had donated to The Little Light House a total of ninety dozen donuts, enough to last for months. And it was one week to the day after I had chided myself for thinking that God would care about such a trivial matter as donuts!

Let him have all of your worries and cares, for he is always thinking about you and watching everything that concerns you. (1 Peter 5:7)

OUR BEGINNING

The first home for The Little Light House was generously provided on a rent-free basis by the Recreation Center for the Physically Limited. The small facility was outgrown within nine months from the opening of school, but we are grateful to them to this day for the special part they had in our beginning.

OUR PRESENT

In April of 1990, The Little Light House moved into a magnificent 22,000-square-foot facility which was carefully and prayerfully designed to meet the needs of disabled young children and infants. This $2.2 million facility was constructed on a debt-free basis as God miraculously worked through the benevolent spirit of the Tulsa community.

Just a toddler when the doors to The Little Light House first opened, Missy and the ministry grew up together!

Missy went on to attend regular private schools in Tulsa, where she graduated with high honors. Successfully competing with sighted peers, Missy held numerous class offices and leadership positions and was selected for many special awards.

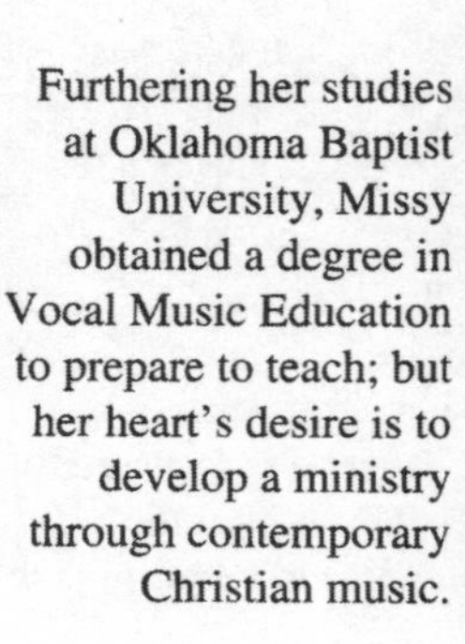

Furthering her studies at Oklahoma Baptist University, Missy obtained a degree in Vocal Music Education to prepare to teach; but her heart's desire is to develop a ministry through contemporary Christian music.

Inspiring the opening of the doors of The Little Light House, Sharmon charmed the hearts of everyone who met her. Though the prognosis was poor at the start, she immediately began achieving milestones that surprised and amazed many professionals.

Though Sharmon struggles with health problems, she continues to display remarkable courage. Her love for the Lord is a precious testimony and a beautiful inspiration for those who are blessed enough for their lives to be touched by hers.

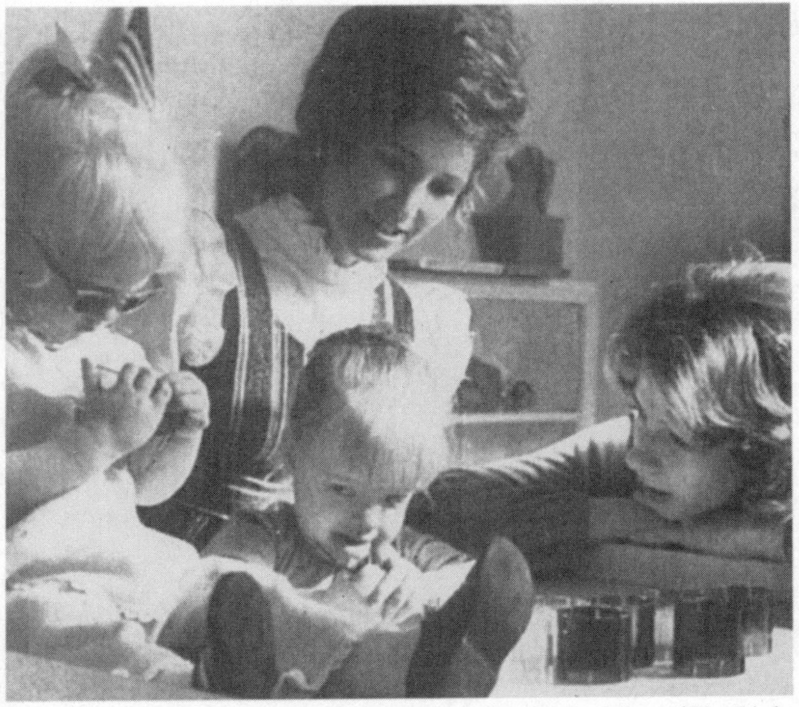

Sheryl and Sharmon and Missy and me, soon after the founding of The Little Light House.

Kristi, the very first teacher ever hired by The Little Light House, laid the foundation and served as the inspiration for all the teachers and therapists who would follow her example of dedication in future years.

Delores, one of the first five volunteers ever to serve at The Little Light House, is still giving of her time faithfully every week as she assists in the classrooms.

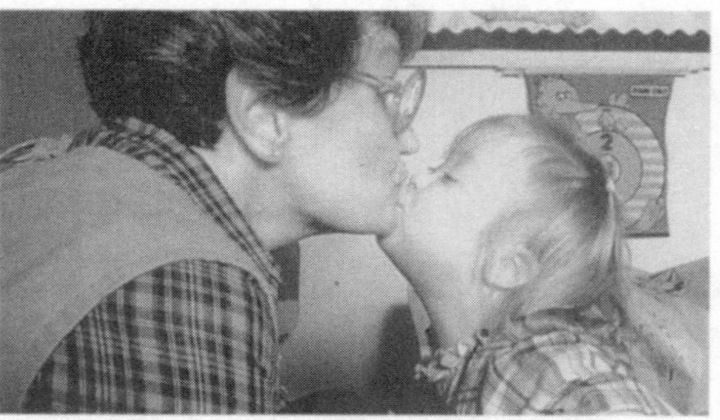

Betty, another one of our long-time faithful classroom volunteers, receives a big kiss, and a lot of love from a Little Light House pupil.

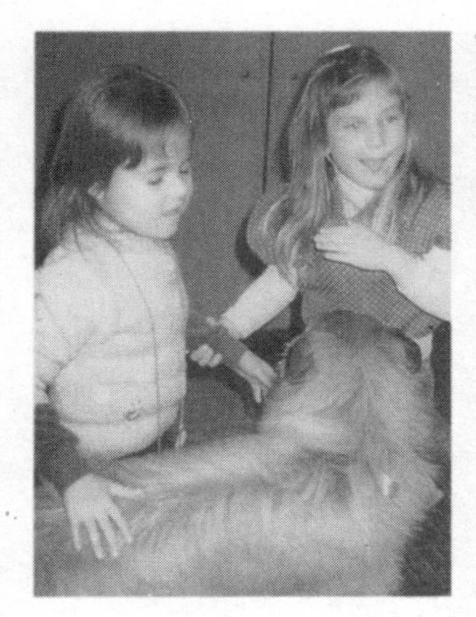

These little girls (former Little Light House pupils) were inseparable. One was totally blind and the other had a significant hearing loss. Together, they provided a living demonstration that love has no language barriers.

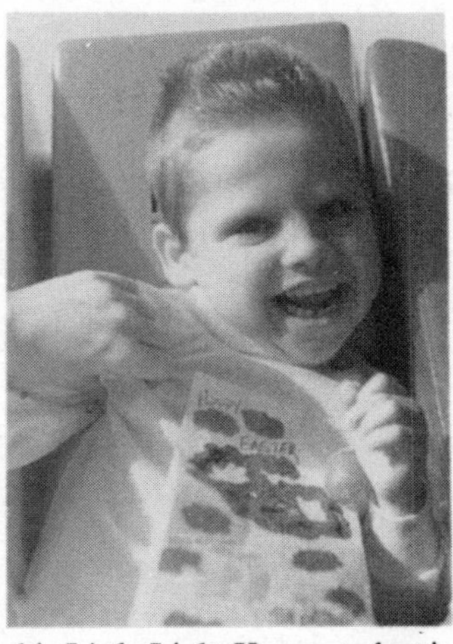

"I can do all things through Christ who strengthens me." (Philippians 4:13, NKJV)

Although this Little Light House student is physically disabled and non-verbal, he has been taught to communicate his needs by "eye gazing" at communication pictures which function as his vocabulary.

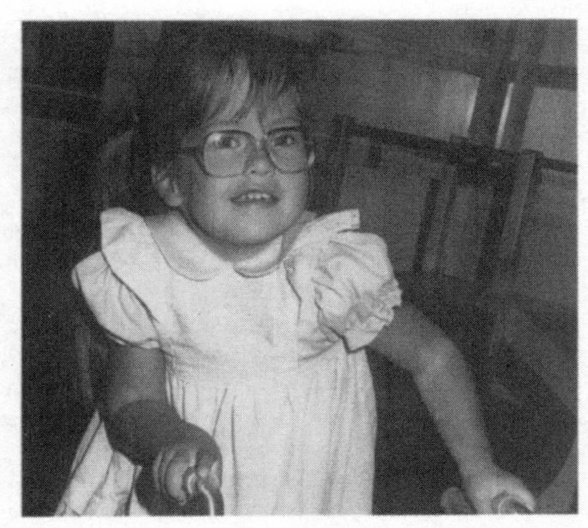

Our little ones grasp the meaning of Philippians 4:13 early in life as they pour their hearts into overcoming the challenges they face.

This moving article, written by Marshall Shelley, editor of "Leadership Magazine," beautifully captures God's heart and purpose for special children like so many served at The Little Light House. It is reprinted here with permission from "Leadership Magazine."

CAN SOMEONE WHO CAN'T SEE, HEAR, OR TALK BE "SUCCESSFUL IN MINISTRY"?

One of the most effective evangelists I've ever met was a child who never uttered a word.

• • •

Mandy was born into our family two years ago, severely and profoundly retarded due to microcephaly. At first we desperately prayed that Mandy would develop some skills, but my wife, Susan, and I eventually had to accept the implications: Mandy would never talk, walk, sit up or use her hands.

She suffered frequent seizures. She stopped swallowing, so we learned to administer medications and formula through a tube surgically implanted into her stomach . . . we never knew if she could see or hear.

Yet, despite her handicaps, Mandy had an amazing ability to elicit love and point people's thoughts to God.

In our congregation, Mandy quickly became "the church's kid." When we would arrive, several sets of arms would reach out to take her. After a service, we had to hunt for her as she'd been passed from lap to lap.

In the neighborhood, the school, or the support group at Easter Seals, she steered conversations. You couldn't be in her presence without thoughts turning a spiritual direction. *Why was such a child born? What is her future? Where does the strength come from to care for her?*

We had no easy answers, but for all these questions, God, resurrection, and support from God's people figured naturally into the only answers that came close to making any sense at all.

One hospital employee, after observing Mandy, said she decided "to get God into my life."

A young boy prayed his very first prayer out loud – for Mandy.

In February, 1992, Mandy suffered a viral pneumonia her body didn't have the strength to shake. Despite our prayers and the physicians' treatments, I began to suspect we would never bring her home.

On Thursday afternoon, Susan and

I sat in Mandy's room, taking turns holding her. A procession of people came by to visit:

A colleague from work, who said: "I don't have anything to say. I just sensed I needed to be near Mandy."

A hospital volunteer, there ostensibly to comfort us, who suddenly poured out the story of her divorce, remarriage, and feeling of estrangement from God, but now her desire to renew her relationship with Him.

Another health-care professional, who uncharacteristically broke into tears. She told us of growing up in a boarding school, away from her missionary parents, and never being openly angry at them but never feeling close to them (or God). Now, after caring for Mandy, longing to regain intimacy with both heavenly and earthly father.

I sat amazed. My child was dying, but in her presence, we experienced revival, confessing sins and drawing near to God.

That night at 7 p.m., Mandy left her "earthly tent" for one "not built by human hands."

In the weeks that followed, even as we grieved her absence, we continued to hear of her influence.

One man I'd always considered uninterested in church wrote us:

"I never held Mandy, though I occasionally stroked her cheek while my wife held her. But I learned a lot from her . . . after seeing Mandy's effect on people, if God can use someone like her, maybe He can use an empty well like me."

Could a sightless, wordless, helpless infant ever be "successful in ministry?" If success is fulfilling God's purposes, I consider Mandy wildly successful.

Can a ministry that's cut short be blessed by God? Mandy's earthly ministry lasted less than two years, but it touched eternity.

And I suspect that's where real success is measured.

Shannon, a Little Light House pupil for eight years, is one of many "effective little evangelists" at The Little Light House and around the world.

Trustees representing five benevolent-minded foundations along with two past Little Light House Board Chairmen are recognized at the dedication of the new permanent home-site of The Little Light House.

Little Light House children and volunteers gather for an "all-school picture" in front of our beautiful new facility.

Pupils assist in the ground-breaking for the playgrounds which were donated by the Rotary Clubs of Tulsa and designed with special children in mind by landscape architect Greg Warren (pictured far right next to his daughter, Meghan, who was a pupil here at The Little Light House at the time).

Children giggle with delight as they swing and play on our specially adaptive playground equipment.

Adaptive teaching aids serve as motivational tools and assist children in developing fine motor skills.

A speech pathologist utilizes special training in oral motor skills to assist a child in developing his ability to chew.

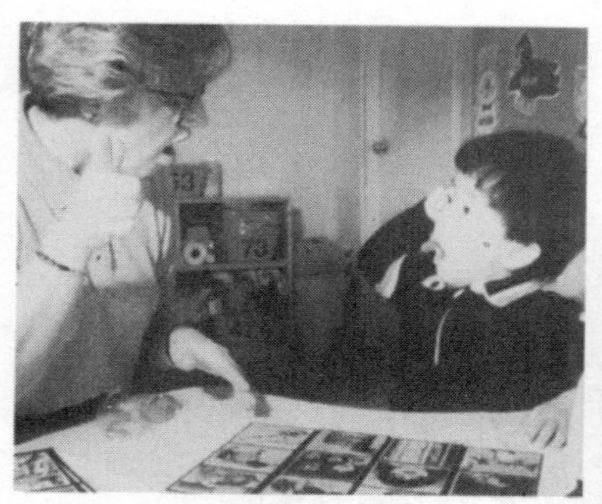

A child who is hearing-impaired learns to use "signing" to communicate.

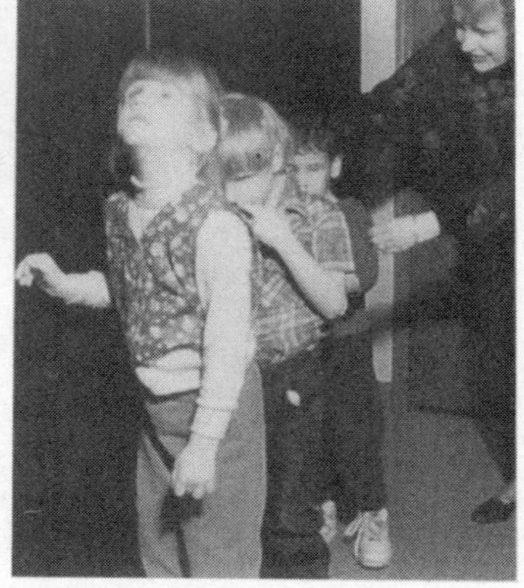

Children visually impaired from birth develop their mobility and orientation skills as they learn to move independently through the center.

Our school nurse, Miss Sherry, provides tender, loving professional care to Little Light House children.

Therapy equipment provided by donors from the community is of great value to Little Light House physical and occupational therapists.

In the pre-kindergarten class, a little girl with cerebral palsy listens closely to her teacher as they work on reading skills.

Parents are an integral part of The Little Light House team as we work together to help their children progress. Parents of Little Light House children assist in countless volunteer capacities and assist in fundraising year round.

State-of-the-art computer equipment with special adaptations is a treasured aide to teachers and therapists.

Frequently, we hear it said by volunteers, staff and parents: "These children bless us far more than we can bless them." How true!

Our teachers offer lots of love and encouragement to our "little ones" as they strive to reach the finish line.

The students of The Little Light House participate in our annual fund raiser, "Mini-Laps," a smaller version of our major fund raiser, "Laps for Little Ones."

As we witness our children progressing from wheelchairs to walkers, and from braces to canes, we all rejoice in their development and thank God for the milestones they are achieving.

GRADUATION!

One of our little graduates and me following the "pomp and circumstance" of a Little Light House graduation ceremony.

Two of our treasured volunteers with President George Bush, after he selected The Little Light House as his 536th Point of Light.

Medallion presented to The Little Light House at a reception held for Point of Light recipients at Disney World in Orlando, Florida.

"Abba, Father"

This beautiful sculpture which graces the entrance of The Little Light House was sculpted by Rosalind Cook, a long-time friend of my own and The Little Light House.

"See how very much our heavenly Father loves us, for he allows us to be called his children." (1 John 3:1)

This simple and yet profound statement is the inspiration for "Abba, Father." "Abba" is an Aramaic term similar to our word "Daddy," which suggests intimacy and an unconditional love.

Though many of the children of The Little Light House are not able to run or see as the child depicted in "Abba, Father," their spirits were created to know of God's love for them. This great love reaches out to each of us. Just as a little child runs confidently into the arms of her father, "Abba, Father" depicts the joy, expectancy and trust we can have as children of God.

". . . because you are sons, God has sent forth the Spirit of His Son into your hearts, crying out, 'Abba, Father!'" (Galatians 4:6, NKJV)

If you would like to enter into this precious relationship with our heavenly Father, you need only pray this prayer . . .

Heavenly Father,
I want you to come into my heart. I acknowledge and confess the wrong and the sin in my life and turn from this sin as I humbly ask your forgiveness. I acknowledge that your Son, Jesus Christ, died for my sins that I might have eternal life and I now profess Him as my Lord and Savior. From this moment on, I relinquish control of my life to you, asking you to guide my thoughts, direct my plans and teach me the way that I should go. I thank you, precious Lord, for this marvelous gift of salvation.
Amen.

16
Cream Off the Top

As The Little Light House grew, so did my love and appreciation for the many precious saints God used to keep the school in operation. Many of them were living testimonies of the teachings of Christ. There were countless individuals who allowed God to work through them to help us in our work — through their time, talents and finances. There was one man in particular, however, who touched our hearts in such a way that we knew we'd never be the same.

We first met him on a typical day at The Little Light House. Throughout the center, staff and volunteers were busy carrying out individually prescribed activities with the children. I was in my office working.

Suddenly a staff member was at my door. "There's a man asking for you. I tried to help him, but he keeps insisting on seeing the one *in charge*."

Inwardly, I hoped this might be a foundation representative, reviewing the center in consideration for a large grant. I followed her into the hall where I saw an older gentleman straining to catch a glimpse of the children in a nearby classroom.

He was a pleasant-looking fellow, but hardly the picture of a corporate executive or a foundation official. He was plainly dressed in old khaki pants and a threadbare shirt, but there seemed to be a special quality about him. His bald head, plump rosy cheeks, and kind eyes resembled Old Saint Nick himself.

I noticed as he came to greet me that he walked with a decided limp. I wondered how long it had taken him to climb the three flights of stairs to our center.

I tried to forget the worries left behind in my office, and greeted him with a smile. "Hello, sir. How may I help you?"

"Are *you* the one in charge?" he asked, with an element of surprise. Evidently I was not what he was hoping to see, either. I was still in my twenties and hardly the picture of a seasoned executive director.

"Yes, sir, I am."

Resigned to the idea of putting his trust in one so young, he finally disclosed the purpose of his visit. "I've passed by this place several times. I like what you do here, and I'd like to help." With that, he dug deeply into his pants pocket and produced a tiny jar filled with coins – nickels, dimes, pennies and quarters. "Here," he said, with warmth in his voice and a twinkle in his eyes. "It's for the kiddies. It's the cream off the top!"

I looked at the small jar, which was about the size of a baby food jar. It couldn't contain more than a couple of dollars' worth of coins, I thought to myself. I was amazed that he would go to so much effort just to bring us a jar full of coins! Still, my heart was touched by his tender spirit.

Hoping he couldn't read my thoughts, I thanked him for his thoughtfulness and invited him to tour the center.

He hesitated only a second and then quickly agreed. As we toured the classrooms, the love that our new friend had in his heart for the children was immediately evident. Every line on his face registered his genuine compassion and concern.

Several days went by before the old man returned. Once again, he climbed the long flight of stairs to pay a personal visit. Once again, he came bearing gifts. This time he placed in my hand a crisp twenty-dollar bill. As before, he told me, "It's for the kiddies. It's the cream off the top, you know! And," he continued, "I have something else for you." With great pride, he reached into his pocket and brought out several small acorns. Leaning over, he whispered, "I found them, polished them, and varnished them myself! Beauties, aren't they? They're for the kiddies, too." I was moved by the beauty he discovered in something as simple as a tiny acorn.

He came repeatedly in the months that followed. The purpose of each visit was always the same — to present more gifts for the "kiddies." Little did we realize what a gift the visits themselves were.

We eventually learned that our special friend had been fitted with an artificial leg, hence the limp. Maneuvering those stairs was no small feat for him. But he insisted on bringing his gifts in person. He never told us much about himself; however, we did learn he had lost his leg due to complications from diabetes and that he had been searching unsuccessfully for a job for quite some time. His age and his disability proved to be overwhelming obstacles for him. I soon learned that his inability to find work bothered him greatly, but he seemed to make the best of his lot. His positive attitude, in fact, was inspiring to all of us.

Once when he was lacking funds, he presented us with S & H Green Stamps he'd received when purchasing gas for his dilapidated old car. Sometimes he brought jewelry for the staff that he had made from small stones he found in a park near his home. He never came empty-handed. And he always left our hearts full!

The Little Light House staff members grew to love this special friend. We looked forward to his cheery face, his joyful spirit and his loving ways.

When a couple of months had passed without our seeing him, we grew concerned. He had never given us his address or phone number, so we had no way of contacting him. We prayed for his safety and well-being.

Then, just as suddenly as he had appeared the first time, he appeared again. With a gift in his hand, he explained he had been in the hospital undergoing tests on his heart.

"You know what?" he said, with that twinkle we'd all come to love. "They proved I've got a ticker!"

But we already knew that.

When the Christmas holidays were upon us, we once again were concerned. Our friend hadn't come around for quite some time. At last, I received a call from him. He explained that his financial reserves had been depleted, and his Social Security check hadn't arrived. Consequently, he had no money for gas, or for "the kiddies." He felt so bad about not being able to bring gifts for the children at Christmas time.

Nothing I said seemed to ease the burden he felt. I asked him if he had everything he needed.

"Oh, of course," he replied. "The Lord is my shepherd. He takes care of me. I have food and medication to last me at least three or four more days. I'm in great shape. I just wanted you and the kiddies to know why you hadn't heard from me. I'll be back to see you before long."

Though it was difficult, I did manage to acquire his address before our conversation ended. After placing a few calls to board and staff members, a unanimous decision was made to deliver a Christmas blessing to this one who had shared so much love with us! Gifts were quickly purchased and wrapped and a date was set to visit him.

It was a frigid December night when we delivered his Christmas basket and learned his well-kept secret – the reason he had been reluctant to reveal his residence. His home was an abandoned, converted schoolbus. His only heat came from the flames of an old gas cook stove. A worn mattress lay in the back where the bus seats had once been located.

Though quite humbled and a bit embarrassed by our visit to his "home," he was, nonetheless, moved by the Christmas gifts and goodies and the love we brought with us. There was barely room for the four of us to stand in the narrow bus. We had entered single file, and since I was the first one on, I was the last to leave. As we turned to go, our friend caught my hand and squeezed a crisp, twenty-dollar bill into my palm. "I got my Social Security check today," he told me. "I want to give the cream off the top to the kiddies."

"But —" I started to protest, with tears forming in my eyes. "Please," he said. "It's Christmas! And it's important to me."

Not long after the holidays, our friend visited us for the last time. In the spring he moved into a heavenly mansion where he resides today. His memory and the selfless life he lived while he was with us, will forever remain in our hearts.

> Then a poor widow came by and dropped in two small copper coins. "Really," he [Jesus] remarked, "this poor widow has given more than all the rest of them combined. For they have given a little of what they didn't need. But she, poor as she is, has given everything she has." (Luke 21:2-4)

17
Where Are You, Lord?

Within months after we had first opened the doors of The Little Light House, we realized it would be only a short time before we would need additional teachers. Later we contacted the public school system in our area and asked about possible funding assistance, but we were turned down.

As our school continued to grow, it became obvious that Kristi would be unable to manage the ever-increasing teaching load alone. We had found ourselves desperately in need of additional staff. Following our move into the church, the same public school official who had turned us down, ended up paying us an unexpected visit.

"This program has come a long way," he said, following his tour of the entire operation. "In fact, it's amazing how far it has come in one year." He paused briefly, then proceeded on in a business-like tone. "As you may know, our public school system has received funding to provide services to deaf-blind children in this area. Some of the children you are now serving are in that category. There are others out in the community who need the kind of services you offer. We certainly can't improve upon the quality of your program. How about letting us provide salaries for additional staff, and we'll arrange for you to provide services to these additional children?"

He continued, "We'll simply put them on our register and send them to you. You can have complete autonomy. This will enable the school system to fulfill its legal obligation and at the same time allow you to expand your staff."

It was precisely what we had requested of him just months before. It *appeared* that God had intervened. Additional staff would mean relief for Kristi from her enormous workload – an answer to our prayers – or so it seemed.

I was somewhat concerned about the issue of the separation of church and state. Could it become a problem? (I was troubled by the thought.) Still, the prospect of increased staff overshadowed my concern. The arrangements would also mean physical and speech therapy services for our pupils.

It didn't take long for our board of directors to act on the matter. By December of 1973, the arrangement with the school system had gone into effect. The direct impact of the agreement came quickly and dramatically to our young school.

Children with all types of disabling conditions became eligible for enrollment. The increase in our pupil population and staff had a mushrooming effect on the scope of our operation. By January of 1976, it had grown to overwhelming proportions. The arrangement appeared to be beneficial to all concerned.

Then, without warning, clouds of discontent began to form, threatening the agreement between the public school system and The Little Light House.

A few sets of parents who had formerly been more than satisfied with the agreement began making demands on public school officials. They insisted on longer school days and expanded services. Some demanded that prayer be eliminated from the classrooms along with the use of Bible stories, songs and posters.

Most of the contention arose out of attempts to operate a public program within a private setting. The standards and policies differed between the two entities, and there was a marked contrast in our philosophies. Influenced by the needs of their children and their own emotional and spiritual struggles, a small percentage of our parents exerted more and more pressure on public school officials to meet their demands. Eventually, these parents succeeded in their efforts.

Left with no other alternative, school administrators reluctantly presented an ultimatum to our board. Program expansions would have to take place within designated time periods. Our administration would have to operate within guidelines set forth by the state.

Prayer and Bible stories were to be eliminated from the classrooms. These and other restrictions pointed to a disintegration of Little Light House autonomy.

The issue of how to respond to the demands of the public school system was the focal point of our next board of directors meeting. Our board members were well aware of the gravity of their decision. Should they elect not to comply with the school district's demands, it would result in loss of funding, cutback of services, and reduction of staff. Considering how dependent we had become on the funding and staff we were receiving from the state, it could even mean the closing of The Little Light House.

If our board of directors was to comply, it would mean a compromise in our commitment to Christ, as well as to the educational standards we had embraced since the founding. The meeting lasted long into the night. Motives and goals were challenged and scrutinized. Issues were examined. All hearts searched to hear from God.

At the close of the meeting, it was decided by a majority vote that The Little Light House would stand firm as a Christ-centered school committed to combining prayer with professional expertise in an effort to minister as effectively as possible to God's special children.

We braced ourselves for the repercussions we knew our decision would evoke. The resolution stunned the very individuals who had raised the initial complaints. The decision of our board was not the result they had hoped for, or anticipated.

At the end of the spring term, school officials withdrew all state-supported funding, staff and equipment just as they indicated they would. Group pressure from parents, and fear that The Little Light House would close, prompted over eighty percent of our parents to transfer their children into quickly developed public school programs. Our enrollment dropped to the size it had been when we first opened our doors.

Over the next year and a half, community donations dwindled, the financial picture darkened and staff morale sank. It was during this same period that

Public Law 94-142 was passed (requiring public school districts to provide a "free and appropriate education to every handicapped child within the least restrictive setting").

Even though a few families continued to seek our services, the whole reason for the school's existence seemed in question. Public schools would now be forced to provide the services we had been providing. Perhaps it was time to close our doors. All of our efforts, hopes and dreams over the past few years seemed to have been shattered. There appeared to be no point in continuing this work we had been so sure God had called us to do.

I became more distraught and confused with every passing day. One morning I wept all the way to work. I prayed as I cried, but my prayers were filled with questions and grievances. When I arrived, I poured out my heart in a letter to God:

> Lord, why did you even begin this work? So much has been poured into it, by the community, the volunteers and the families of the children.
>
> A few families still want and need our services. But there are too few of them to justify the continuation of The Little Light House. Lord, if you give us one reason, one real, tangible reason to remain open, we'll continue. We might be tired and struggling today, but I know you can give us strength. Help us to understand the purpose in continuing.

The board of directors shared my anguish. The loss of state funding had a devastating effect on our finances. That fact, coupled with the implications of the new law, *seemed* to be bringing an end to the dream school that once was *so* needed, and seemed so divinely appointed.

At one point, the closing of The Little Light House seemed so inevitable and God seemed so far away, that at the time I journaled:

> Lord, I wish the waiting were over. With so few children left to serve, I've no incentive to carry on with this work. I don't understand why you created this work for such a short season. Yet, visible factors point to that. How are we to tell currently enrolled families and staff who desire a Christian school that the center will be closing? What are we to do with the equipment and the furniture? A solution to this dilemma seems impossible! Lord, *please* show us what you want us to do.

My heart cried out for wisdom. My mind searched for answers and my spirit ached to hear from God. If only He would answer. Yet all I heard was silence.

> For I know the plans I have for you, says the Lord. They are plans for good and not for evil, to give you a future and a hope. In those days when you pray, I will listen. You will find me when you seek me, if you look for me in earnest. (Jeremiah 29:11-13)

18
Tightening Our Budget and Stretching Our Faith

God remained silent. In the ensuing months, precious children with special needs that weren't being met with state-supported programs began making their way to The Little Light House. Our enrollment began to grow again, but within three months of the cutoff of state funding, the center's small financial reserve was depleted. Though we continued to receive contributions, they were hardly enough to support our budget.

In darker moments, we considered charging tuition. However, even a minimal fee of ten dollars per month had proven to be more than many families could pay. These families had never planned to have children who would require such extensive medical care. Few were prepared for the financial devastation brought on all too often by such circumstances. Each time we reevaluated the issue of tuition, we arrived at a stronger conclusion that we were to offer the services tuition-free and further demonstrate the love of Christ.

Our overall financial statement grew more dismal with every passing day. Months earlier, our staff had been alerted to the financial challenges the center was likely to face. They were given a choice to transfer into the public school program or to remain with The Little Light House. To stay would obviously involve a giant step of faith on their part. There was no guarantee our school would even continue. Still, most of our staff members chose to stay.

Their loyalty raised ambivalent feelings as our board considered a new dilemma. With the drop in enrollment, we couldn't justify the need for all the staff who chose to stay. We couldn't pay them for long, and yet we didn't have the heart to dismiss them. We asked God for guidance.

We received clear direction. The Little Light House was to retain all who chose to stay until God led them elsewhere.

Subsequently, one staff member's husband was transferred out of state by his company, another staff member married and moved away, and still another left to have a baby. Several months later, only a few staff members remained. God had divinely reduced the number to an appropriate size.

The decrease in staff radically lessened our monthly expenses. Still, we sought every conceivable way to trim the budget even more. We knew our reduced revenue could not keep up with the demands of our operating needs for very long.

It didn't. Each month, following the payment of bills and payroll, the bank balance dropped lower than the month before. Finally that which I had feared most came to pass.

Nancy, our secretary and bookkeeper, stopped by my office. Her face spoke a thousand words. She announced, "We have a serious problem." Then she hesitated briefly, not wanting to continue. "There's not enough in our account to pay the staff as well as the bills today! What do you want me to do?"

I felt a knot growing in my stomach. "Have you double-checked your figures?"

She nodded. "Several times."

We had seen this shortfall coming and we had done everything we knew to avoid it.

"How much do we lack?"

"A little over $350."

Finances had always been tight, but never before had we lacked adequate funds to pay our bills and our staff on time.

"Well," I said resolutely, "we'll just pray! God knows our need exists. We'll just ask Him to provide the sum we need by the close of the day. He can do that!"

As she left, I wished my heart had been as confident as I knew my voice had sounded. I closed the door to my office. "O Lord," I prayed. "Help us. Please send us the money we need before 4:00 today!" For the rest of the day, those prayerful words weren't far from my mind or my lips.

Still, I was as amazed as Nancy was when a donor stopped by and, for no explainable reason, hand-delivered a contribution of $400. Perhaps, I thought, God was trying to stretch our faith.

Over the next few months that scene repeated itself numerous times. Funds arrived hours, sometimes minutes before a critical need had to be met. I wondered if this was God's way of keeping our eyes focused on Him. I sensed, however, it was more than that.

October 31 of 1976 will be etched in my memory forever. The day was not unlike any other day when funds were low. However, this time we were more than just a few hundred dollars shy from being able to pay our bills and staff. We were over $3,000 short!

Utilizing most of what we had in our account, we could cover all the bills. But the amount remaining would enable us to pay only a few of our staff.

We had never been delinquent on our bill payments. I couldn't imagine that God would want that. "But then," I reasoned, "surely God wouldn't want the staff to go unpaid either."

I had been sitting in my office for hours, poring over the books, my faith drained out of me.

"I don't understand, Lord! I just don't understand." We all had a sense that God wanted us to continue reaching out to the children He had called us to minister to. And yet, to do that we needed financial provision. If we were going to carry on the work, I wanted with all my heart for it to glorify God. I failed to see how this dreadful financial predicament could be to His glory!

As I prayed that afternoon, I vented hot, angry words at God, until finally the prayers turned into long, uncontrollable sobs. There seemed to be no answers — only the same devastating silence.

Finally, I called Phil at work. He knew immediately there were serious problems. "What's wrong, hon?"

I tearfully related the whole situation to him. I could sense his feeling of helplessness.

"I don't know what to tell you," he said. Then his voice brightened a bit. "How about calling Ed? Being board treasurer, maybe he'll have some advice." Then he added, "Who knows, maybe the funds will still come in today. We've seen it happen before!"

I knew that was true. But something felt different about this day.

Ed shared my concern, but wasn't able to give me direction either. Later, I talked with our board chairman and two or three others whose counsel I respected. Each offered words of consolation, but still I lacked direction. "Lord, please tell me what to do!" I pleaded.

The mail brought only a few dollars. There were no surprise visitors bringing substantial donations that day. As the afternoon drew to a close, the center's financial status remained unchanged.

It was time to join the staff for prayer. Moments before I headed down the long hall to join the others, God spoke to my heart.

He brought to mind the choice the staff had made to remain with The Little Light House. They knew it would be a faith walk. But the vendors who billed us for services and goods had made no such commitment.

As vendors, they were expecting to be paid. It seemed our priority must be to pay them. Still, my heart went out to the staff. "Lord, what about them?" I prayed. "The Bible promises you'll meet the needs of your children."

That's when that still, small voice said simply, "*I will. Trust me.*" As I walked down the hall, my heart was strongly impressed with what I was to say to the staff.

I felt a strange peace as I joined them. They sat quietly and expectantly as I entered the small room. It was evident; they sensed my burden.

"There's something I need to share with you," I began.

It took only a few moments to share our financial position. I told them of my prayers for guidance and explained the direction I believed God had placed on my heart.

"I believe we are to pay our bills first. Trusting God to meet the needs of the staff, I believe we can count on having enough left over after paying the bills to pay those who really need to receive checks today and enough in the days to come to pay the others as their needs require. However, because this is a decision that could have an impact on your lives and because I believe God gives confirmation to His direction, I have something to ask of you."

I handed out small sheets of paper to each one and then said, "I'd like you to pray silently, asking God to tell *you* what He would have us do. Please don't share your thoughts aloud. Then write the answer to these two questions on your paper.

"First, do *you* believe God is directing us to pay the center's bills, or use our funds toward payroll? Second, do you personally need your check today in order for your immediate needs to be met?"

Then I cautioned, "If you need your check today, please be honest and say so." I suspected that honesty was likely a common denominator in God's mathematics.

I waited. There was a hush over the room as they prayed. A short while later, one by one, they folded their papers and passed them to me. Finally, the last one was in my hand. I breathed a silent prayer and began to read each one. The first read, "Pay bills first. I don't need my check." The next was the same, as was the next. Then, I came to one that stated, "Pay bills first. I don't need my check today, but I do need $100 to pay my rent." The next one read, "Pay bills first. I don't need my check. And I have $100 if anyone is in a tight spot."

By the time I read the last one, tears clouded my eyes. Only a few stated they needed their checks. All the notes stated we should pay the bills first.

With a lump in my throat, I returned to my office to calculate the payroll checks which had been requested. We had just enough to cover the bills, pay each one who expressed a need to receive a check that day, and to keep the bank account open.

As I drove home that evening, I reflected over the long day. I had been so concerned about how our predicament could bring glory to God. "I think I understand now, Lord. As these staff members trust you to meet their needs, as they put you first and continue to reach out to these special children as you have called them to – you *are* glorified!"

I had always been fearful of what might happen under the circumstances we had faced that day. At last I knew. God was still at work. My faith was still intact. And He was definitely in control.

So don't worry at all about having enough food and clothing. Why be like the heathen? For they take pride in all these things and are deeply concerned about them. But your heavenly Father already knows perfectly well that you need them, and he will give them to you if you give him first place in your life and live as he wants you to. So don't be anxious about tomorrow. God will take care of your tomorrow too. Live one day at a time. (Matthew 6:31-34)

19

Without Words, They Teach

Although we didn't know how long the doors of The Little Light House would remain open, we did know that as long as they were open, we wanted to operate the school within the heart of God's perfect will. We asked Him to redefine our vision and restructure and revamp The Little Light House to His divine specifications.

It was at this time that we began to understand our calling. God wanted us to be more than a school. He had called us to be His ministry – ministering in the name of Jesus Christ, not only to the educational and developmental needs of His special children, but to their spiritual needs as well.

The words in Matthew 5:16 best describe the purpose God was redefining for our ministry. "Let your light so shine before men, that they may see your good works and give glory to your Father who is in heaven" (Revised Standard Version). Our corporate papers, goals, logo and brochures were all changed to reflect that calling.

Our enrollment continued to grow slowly. Even though most parents were attracted to the solidity and security which the federally funded programs seemed to offer, there were those who were drawn to the individualized approach of The Little Light House and valued the Christian atmosphere they found within our doors.

Those children who had remained with us, and the new ones who came, were there to grow and learn — to be taught. Yet, as we viewed these little ones through God's perspective, they became the teachers.

One of the first to be added to our small enrollment was a bouncy, bubbly little girl with a pixie face. Shortly after she came to us, Christy lost both of her eyes as a result of tumors.

She became best friends with an adorable, energetic child named Kim, who was born with a profound hearing loss. The two had no means of communicating with each other. Kim couldn't hear Christy speaking, and Christy couldn't see Kim hand-signing. Yet, they were inseparable. Daily they taught us that love has no barriers.

Two brothers, both totally blind from birth, quickly won their way into our hearts. One was four and the other was nine months old when they were first enrolled. As these two went through their daily routines, relying on the loving volunteers and staff to help them overcome their fears of open space and startling sounds, we learned a deeper meaning for the word "trust."

And then there was our sweet Stephanie, a fragile little brunette, who suffered from a brain tumor. Everyone who came in contact with this child grasped the real meaning of the word "courage."

There were other "little teachers" who followed. We often wondered how it was that they gave us so much more than we ever gave them.

Some even taught without words. Such was the case with a little boy who couldn't speak, yet led his parents in a dinnertime blessing. As his parents later related to us, when they were called out of town, they asked two of our staff to babysit with their son for a week. Each evening, when they gathered at the dinner table, the two teachers and the child joined hands, bowed their heads and prayed a blessing over the meal. Night after night they prayed together in the same manner.

The first evening after his parents returned home, they sat down for dinner with him and began to eat. They were just getting ready to take their first bite when the small child reached over and insisted on holding his daddy's and mother's hands.

"What is it?" the parents asked. "You want us to hold hands? Right now?"

The little guy smiled. Finally they took his hands. Then to their amazement, he began to bob his head up and down. Finally the parents concluded, "The teachers must have held hands, bowed their heads, and said a blessing with him while we were gone. He is wanting us to say a blessing!" So all three bowed their heads. Then, watching his reaction, one of his parents began to say a prayer.

Suddenly, the little guy released his grip on his daddy's hand and reached over and gently touched each of his daddy's eyelids, and then those of his mother.

"I guess he wants us to close our eyes to pray," his mother responded tenderly. And so, a new tradition was born as the small family held hands and bowed their heads and prayed a blessing over their meal.

Jesus called a small child over to him and set the little fellow down among them, and said,"Unless you turn to God from your sins and become as little children, you will never get into the Kingdom of Heaven. Therefore anyone who humbles himself as this little child, is the greatest in the Kingdom of Heaven.And any of you who welcomes a little child like this because you are mine, is welcoming me and caring for me." (Matthew 18:2-5)

20

When There's No Answer – Don't Hang Up!

The spring of 1977 brought many changes. We were without the public school financial assistance we had relied upon so heavily for three years.

Kristi married a handsome young seminary student and moved away from Tulsa. Sharmon's parents also relocated outside of the Tulsa area. Missy graduated from The Little Light House and entered kindergarten. I felt unsettled with all the changes that were taking place and still uncertain about the future.

Over the next year our vision of what God was calling us to grew even clearer. The blessings we received from the children were even greater, but our financial problems worsened. We continued to pray for supplies and equipment, but tangible answers to prayer were less frequent. Staff members grew accustomed to voluntarily giving up a timely receipt of their paychecks to ensure that all ministry bills be paid. Somehow, I felt responsible for the sacrifices they made.

These problems, combined with the changes taking place and the emotional strain of the past months, had wrought a cumulative and negative effect on my spiritual state.

I longed for the days when we prayed for smocks, donuts and toys and they miraculously appeared. I yearned for the kind of dramatic miracles we had once seen on a daily basis in the early days of the ministry.

"Please, Lord," I pleaded one morning. "I feel my faith is slipping. I can't go on without visible evidence of your love."

God remained silent.

"Lord, you know we have taken a difficult stand," I cried out. "Now, it appears you have forgotten us."

Several days passed. Still there was no sign of the Master's hand, no obvious divine intervention, no tangible evidence of His presence or His love.

My faith level spiraled further and further downward. Eventually, I began to take the whole matter personally. I begged Him to send someone or to provide a physical sign that proved He was hearing my plea — that He still loved us, that His hand was still on this work He had called us to do.

In the days that followed, not once did I sense that anyone was on a mission from God to assure me of His love or to prove that He was still watching over The Little Light House.

In the leadership position of this struggling ministry, I felt personally rejected, abandoned, used, broken and forgotten. Finally, in a state of defeat, I gave up. I stopped praying.

During the next few weeks, I sank further into depression. At the center, I called on others to pray during flock rather than leading the prayer myself. When it was my responsibility to lead the Bible study or give the devotion, I gave reasons why I couldn't and assigned it to others. I'll never know whether the other staff members realized the extent of the spiritual battle that was raging within me.

Every day seemed worse than the one before. Gone were the days when I experienced moment-by-moment, day-by-day, sweet fellowship with the Lord.

Weeks passed. I remained hurt and angry. I knew He was there. But why wasn't He answering my prayers as He had in the early days of the ministry?

I felt a spiritual numbness, an emptiness and a tremendous sense of loss. I wanted once again to experience an intimate fellowship with my Savior, but I thought it was too late. Surely in turning away from Him, I had been guilty of all but blaspheming God.

The spiritual barrenness continued for several weeks, until one night in desperation, I lay crying on my bed. "O God! I need you back. I don't care about all the physical manifestations of your love or what you do or don't do for me or The Little Light House. It's your ministry and I'm your child to do with as you will. I just want you — to fellowship with you and to love you. Please let me feel your presence in my heart once again. Please just speak to me."

In a state of emotional and spiritual exhaustion, I fell asleep. When I awoke, I was refreshed and felt more alive than I had in weeks. As I prepared for the day, a thought came to me: "If you didn't hear from your closest friend for a long period of time, would you assume she no longer cared and no longer wanted to be with you?"

I thought a moment, remembering a dear friend of mine who'd recently moved several hundred miles away. I hadn't heard from her, but I never doubted that she was still my friend. "I'd give her the benefit of the doubt," I reasoned. "I'd assume she had good reason for her silence." Then a thought came to me as clearly as though Phil had spoken it from across the room: "Will you do no less for your Lord?"

"Lord," I asked with an expectant heart, "is that answer from you? Are you saying there was a reason for your silence – that you were there all along, still loving me? But, Lord, why? Why the silence?"

Then I realized that it didn't matter why. I knew I needed Him. And whether He chose to be silent or divinely demonstrative, I would always choose to love Him, to serve Him and to fellowship with Him. When I was ready to know the reason for His silence, He would show me.

> Who then can ever keep Christ's love from us? When we have trouble or calamity, when we are hunted down or destroyed, is it because he doesn't love us anymore? And if we are hungry, or penniless, or in danger, or threatened with death, has God deserted us?
>
> No, for the Scriptures tell us that for his sake we must be ready to face death at every moment of the day – we are like sheep awaiting slaughter; but despite all this, overwhelming victory is ours through Christ who loved us enough to die for us. For I am convinced that nothing can ever separate us from his love. Death can't, and life can't. The angels won't, and all the powers of hell itself cannot keep God's love away. Our fears for today, our worries about tomorrow, or where we are – high above the sky, or in the deepest ocean – nothing will ever be able to separate us from the love of God demonstrated by our Lord Jesus Christ when he died for us. (Romans 8:35-39)

* * *

In the coming days, conditions looked as bleak as ever at The Little Light House, but my heart felt brighter. Still, I wondered why He'd been silent for so long.

One morning as I was reading my Bible, the answer came. During Jesus' life on earth, He performed countless miracles. People were healed, water was turned to wine, food was multiplied, and even the dead were raised to life. But the people pleaded for still *more miracles* until finally Jesus asked them, "Won't any of you believe in me unless I do more and more miracles?" (John 4:48).

At another time Jesus said, "The truth of the matter is that you want to be with me because I fed you, not because you believe in me. But you shouldn't be so concerned about perishable things like food. No, spend your energy seeking the eternal life that I, the Messiah, can give you" (John 6:26-27).

I thought back on all the dramatic miracles we'd witnessed in the early years of ministry. It had been easy to believe then. Not a day went by when we weren't witnessing God's miracle-working power in its most dramatic form!

I read on. Jesus said to Thomas, "You believe because you have seen me. But blessed are those who haven't seen me and believe anyway" (John 20:29).

So that was it! My faith had become dependent upon visible signs and evidence of the power of God. But God wanted to take me into a new dimension of faith — faith that would remain strong when no visible evidence existed.

He was quietly teaching me to put my trust in *Him,* not in His miracles. He was deepening my relationship with himself and guiding me to a new understanding of love — an unconditional love and surrender — a yieldedness to His sovereign plan! And in the process I learned:

> Even when we are too weak to have any faith left, he remains faithful to us and will help us, for he cannot disown us who are part of himself, and he will always carry out his promises to us. (2 Timothy 2:13)

21
And a Full Tummy Sure Helps!

It wasn't long after I learned the precious and valuable lesson about trusting in God's sovereign plan that we once again began to *see* Him working on a daily basis, but often in unusual ways!

We continued to pray fervently for each month's provision. Although the financial strain seemed to have the greatest ramifications for our staff, they were the very ones whose spirits never faltered. One would have never known that on a voluntary basis they were going without paychecks.

Day in and day out, they modeled the same kind of devotion to God as I had seen evidenced in Kristi's life. Four of our teachers, Jan, Jody, Kate and Bess, had all been a part of the same discipleship program at a local university. It was a program that God used mightily to set their hearts on course. I, along with countless others, benefitted from their sensitivity and obedience to the leadership of God.

They, along with Sheilia, a godly young administrative staff member, often led our flock times. These moments together became more and more meaningful to each staff member. Together we hungered for direction and feasted on God's Word, thankful for the countless practical ways it helped us through that difficult time.

We shared Scriptures which provided comfort in times of stress and difficulty. We encouraged each other with praise reports which reflected ways we had seen God directly and divinely intervene to meet specific needs to accomplish developmental milestones in the lives of the children and spiritual milestones in the lives of the staff.

Such was the time when Jody, our teacher of our hearing-impaired children, ran out of deodorant. "A strange thing to pray for," she thought to herself, and yet surely not too difficult for God to supply! Soon after she began praying, she arrived home to discover a sack of groceries and gifts of clothing on her porch. The sack bore no name of the one who had left it. Only her heavenly Father had heard her petition, but to that, there was no question. For there in the bottom of the sack lay three sticks of deodorant!

All of the staff were young women seeking after the heart of God. They were committed to serving Him — bringing glory to the Master — no matter what the cost. They touched the very depths of my heart as I witnessed their zeal and fervor.

At times I grew concerned for their welfare, however. Typically, we gathered at the end of the school day and chatted over sack lunches. Their lunches became more and more scant due to their lack of income. My concern led me to call Sheryl, who was still serving on our board, even though it meant commuting from out of town. I explained the situation. Sheryl passed the word on to other board members and they were quick to respond.

The next day, after the children had gone home, a board member asked our staff to gather in our flock room. There we found a table covered with grocery sacks, each brimming with all types of needed grocery items — more than enough to provide for every staff member. Each sack was topped with grocery store certificates for meats and additional needed supplies.

On the wall above the table was a sign which read: "This grocery store is free — Jesus paid it all!"

In the center of the sign was a grocery sack decorated with colored sketches drawn by my friend, an artist and board member, Rosalind Cook. The drawing was of children gleefully eating various goodies to their hearts' content! Above the sketch Rosalind had printed: "Man does not live by bread alone, but a full tummy sure helps!" What a joy-packed afternoon that was for our staff.

Funds continued to be scarce, and eventually the staff sought the Lord regarding other ways He might have us meet the needs of fellow staff members. We were particularly concerned about those who were single and had no other sources of income.

One of our staff read in the book of Acts, "All the believers were of one heart and mind, and no one felt that what he owned was his own; everyone was sharing" (Acts 4:32). Our staff took this Scripture to heart.

The staff organized a "Staff Community Grocery Exchange." A list was circulated on which the staff recorded needed items. They would then bring any listed items of which they had extras. Overnight, we saw toothpaste, shampoo, soap and the like being exchanged — a tradition which still exists today, and is carried on for the staff by the parents of The Little

Light House students when funds are low and budgets are tight.

The young women who were so faithful during these difficult times have all gone on to marriages, other careers, or various mission fields. But their legacy lives on. They will never be forgotten.

They were vital workers in laying the foundation on which The Little Light House was built — a foundation which includes a dependency on Jesus Christ, a reliance on Him and His Word for guidance, and a commitment to obedience, no matter what the sacrifice. I will always cherish the friendship of each of these staff members, and I will always be grateful for the effect they had on me personally and, most assuredly, on the entire ministry.

> For the eyes of the Lord search back and forth across the whole earth, looking for people whose hearts are perfect toward him, so that he can show his great power in helping them. (2 Chronicles 16:9)

22
The Fleece

A year and a half passed. To most, the future of The Little Light House continued to appear shaky. Because of the sacrificial spirits of the staff, there were always adequate funds to pay the bills promptly, but it gravely concerned the board when the staff couldn't be paid in a timely manner.

I shared their burden and once again had difficulty dismissing the question of whether the work of The Little Light House should even continue. My mind constantly battled with my heart and my spirit. So much time, money and energy were required to carry on this ministry.

On a daily basis, I asked God for guidance. There were so many contrasts between then and when we first opened the doors of The Little Light House. In 1972 there were no services for the children we had set out to serve. Since then the new law had been passed, requiring public schools to provide services for all disabled children. We knew we offered a Christian alternative and more individualized and specialized services than what most public programs were able to offer, but there still didn't seem to be enough demand for our program to justify the cost and the degree of sacrifice our staff was making.

And, of course, we were faced also with the ongoing bleak financial picture. We must have looked foolish to our community as we continued under such circumstances. Yet, God wouldn't give us a peace about closing.

I wondered if there had ever been a time when God had asked someone else to continue a work even when it didn't make sense from a human point of view. Then I was reminded of Noah.

Surely Noah looked foolish to his fellow men when God called him to build an ark. Most certainly, his efforts were viewed with skepticism. No one had seen a flood. In fact, no one had yet seen rain. In all likelihood, Noah's commitment was scorned, his obedience laughed at – yet he kept building. Undoubtedly, he was ridiculed – yet he remained undaunted. As he progressed with his assignment from God, there was no downpour to douse the doubts of those who observed his persistence.

Unquestionably Noah, too, yearned for God to demonstrate to his world the validity of his mission. What prompted Noah to press on? I found my answer in Hebrews 11:7:

> Noah was another who trusted God. When he heard God's warning about the future, Noah believed him even though there was then no sign of a flood, and wasting no time, he built the ark and saved his family.

Noah simply believed and obeyed God! Was God calling us to the same simple faith and obedience – faith without sight?

Though we couldn't see signs of real need for it at the time, I wondered if God was calling us to prepare an "ark of ministry" for His special children. And if so, could that mean there would be a flood of children in the future who would need our services? It made no sense at the time. Still, if it was an ark God wanted, my heart yearned to obey. "All right, Lord. You provide the courage, and we'll commit to continue!"

But the continuation of the ministry was not my decision alone. This decision legally rested with our board of directors. Finally, the issue was raised at a board meeting. I believed God had finally spoken to my spirit, but would the board receive the same message?

I listened that evening as their discussion became more and more intense regarding whether or not the ministry should continue. The arguments were strong on both sides of the issue. One argued that surely it was wrong for staff members to continue going without regular paychecks. After all, they had been faithful through almost two years of financial drought.

On the other hand, God was blessing the ministry in other ways. None could deny the fact that there were consistent confirmations that pointed to the need for the center to remain open. All bills continued to be paid, and the new families receiving services, though they were not many in number, placed great value in our program.

As they discussed the possibility of closing the center, my thoughts turned to those early days when I had put so much time into its development and survival. During that time, and especially after it became evident that I would need to serve as executive director,

I had lost all sense of priorities as a wife and mother. My family had suffered as a result.

Understandably, Phil had experienced enormous frustration during those years. And although I had long since rearranged my priorities by attempting to always put my family first, he still longed to have me back home full-time.

As the meeting continued, I wondered what Phil's reaction would be. He was in a prime position to influence the decision of whether or not to keep the ministry going. Yet he remained pensive and quiet as other members of the board engaged in lengthy discussion.

Finally, he spoke. "I was there when the doors of The Little Light House first opened. I witnessed twentieth-century miracles as God orchestrated the founding and development of this ministry to special children. There is no doubt in my mind that it has only been by God's grace, provision and appointment that it has survived. It has involved heartache and sacrifice. At times, it was so difficult, I wished the center *would* close."

He paused for just a moment. "But now, I know in my heart I can't be a part of the closing of the very doors that God opened. I can only be a part of such action if we are *certain* it is by His direction!"

It was through Phil's voice that God changed the direction of the entire meeting. From then on, the focus of the conversation changed. The emphasis switched from decision to discernment – from the will of the board to the will of God.

One board member referred to a Scripture in the Old Testament where an angel of the Lord had appeared to Gideon. Gideon was called to the task of saving Israel from the Midianites. He was told that God would be with him. Twice Gideon asked for a miracle to *assure* him that God would be with him. Twice God confirmed the direction:

> Then Gideon said to God, "If you are really going to use me to save Israel as you promised, prove it to me in this way: I'll put some wool on the threshing floor tonight, and if, in the morning, the fleece is wet and the ground is dry, I will know you are going to help me!"
>
> And it happened just that way! When he got up the next morning he pressed the fleece together and wrung out a whole bowlful of water! Then Gideon said to the Lord, "Please don't be angry with me, but let me make one more test: this time let the fleece remain dry while the ground around it is wet!" So the Lord did as he asked; that night the fleece stayed dry, but the ground was covered with dew! (Judges 6:36-40)

Like Gideon, our board needed assurance that God was directing us and would be with us. They needed to know beyond a shadow of a doubt *if it was the will of God* for The Little Light House to remain open. Then and only then could we face the financial giants that loomed in the land ahead.

It was decided we, too, would ask God for assurance that it was His will for us to continue the ministry. Our board knew no other way than to lay a financial "fleece" before the Lord.

They asked God to confirm His will by providing enough funds to enable The Little Light House to keep all bills paid, but also to have the staff completely paid to date by January 1, 1978. We knew this meant the income would have to triple in the coming months — and undoubtedly that would take a miracle.

To be assured that the fleece was being effected only by God, we determined to tell no one of the plan. It was also determined that neither staff members nor board members could personally contribute to the income for that limited amount of time.

I felt partially relieved. Now the board would know for certain of God's plan for the center. And even though I felt in my heart He had directed us to continue, I was thankful for the additional assurance. Truly, it would have to be *God* working for this financial fleece to be answered. I reconciled in my heart and mind that it was God's ministry to open, and His to close.

We watched with amazement as the income slowly increased. We were doing nothing to manipulate the revenue, yet for the first time in eighteen months, the donations were increasing. That trend continued through Christmas. Yet prior to the last mail delivery before January 1, 1978, we still lacked $1,000.

In my mind, it might as well have been one million dollars! I knew, unless we had every dime we needed, our board would rightly interpret the lack as being God's will for us to close the doors.

The center was closed for the New Year's Eve holiday. I drove to the office to open the last of the mail to be delivered prior to January 1, 1978. Six envelopes had been delivered. I sat for several moments with the six envelopes in my hand. I opened the first five. They contained a total of $180. I breathed a sigh of resignation as I whispered, "Lord, the ministry was yours to open; it is yours to close. We just needed to know your will."

Weakly, I opened the last envelope. A check and a letter fell out. The check was made out for $1,000!

Tears flooded my eyes. "O Lord, I *did* understand you correctly. We *are* to continue! Thank you, Lord, for this confirmation. Children will continue to be ministered to through The Little Light House. You do have a purpose for us."

The letter I was holding was from a husband and wife. They had felt strangely impressed to send that exact sum.

Staff members were paid in full and from that day until 1986, the ministry never lacked for adequate funds to cover all financial obligations. Our fleece proved to be a true reflection of God's direction! The waiting had increased our faith and purified our motives. The confirmation of His will strengthened our determination to complete the ark!

And Noah did everything as God commanded him. (Genesis 6:22)

23

God Moves in Mysterious Ways

Once God's will was confirmed to us, the whole ministry began moving forward again. The pupil enrollment began to rise again significantly, bringing about a sudden surge of growing pains. Over the six years in which we had occupied the wing of the church, which had been so generously provided for us, space had never been a problem. However, being located on the third floor was creating increasing difficulties. Elevator access did not exist in our part of the building. Many of our children had grown. Consequently, volunteers, parents and staff carrying non-ambulatory children were exhausted by the time they reached our floor. With every passing day, we became more aware of the risks involved.

As in previous years, we committed the matter to prayer. Once again, God sent a pastor. He had heard of our need for ground-floor space from a member of his congregation at Southside Christian Church. He felt that offering us a new home in their ground-floor wing would be a splendid way to involve their church in outreach and make good use of their facility during the weekdays. We enthusiastically agreed.

The offer was made by the church's board of trustees late in the fall of 1979. Though the existing floor plan was not compatible with the needs of our ministry, the church allowed us to modify the building to our own needs and specifications.

We contacted a dear, little lady who, years before, had designated a generous gift of $27,000 for a future permanent home for The Little Light House. She was more than willing to permit us to use a portion of the funds to remodel the new space.

In coordinating calendars, it became evident that we needed to move during the first week in January. The facility would have to be completely remodeled in a matter of weeks. Walls had to be knocked out, dry walls and observation windows had to be installed. The entire 7,000-square-foot facility required significant renovation and modification. I knew only one man who would take on such a challenge. That special man was Bob Phillips, our good friend who had served as the best man for our wedding.

When I called Bob, I told him I needed a miracle! I gave him the date and described the task. He had a crew together within the week. They worked night and day. When we needed more funds than those we had allocated for the project, Bob approached his Southeast Rotary Club of Tulsa, and they met the need.

The facility was completed on time, and our move was scheduled for the same week. Another group, the North Tulsa Rotarians, volunteered to serve as a moving crew.

The morning we were scheduled to move, we awoke to a weather forecast of sleet "throughout the day over most of Tulsa"! We prayed fervently that God would hold the weather at bay until after our move, and the roads remained dry between the two locations the entire day. The Rotarians still talk about the torrents of sleet that started the minute the last piece of equipment was unloaded. They also recall with wonder the fact that sleet did fall on most of Tulsa much of that same day — except between 3rd and Xanthus and 38th and Lewis — our old and our new locations.

Once again, God proved faithful. The Little Light House was in a rent-free home where we could minister to God's special children for the next ten years.

God's ways are as mysterious as the pathway of the wind. (Ecclesiastes 11:5a)

24
Angels Unaware

As time went on, and the ministry continued to grow, keeping up with the mounting administrative tasks proved to be an ongoing and formidable task. The number of requests for speaking engagements increased by the day.

Normally, I looked forward to sharing with civic groups and other community organizations about The Little Light House. However, on one particular day, there was an unusual overload of work. Consequently, the thought of leaving the center filled me with anxiety. My anxious feelings were heightened by the knowledge that most of the staff was on break. Laura would be the only one there that day to tackle the huge stack of paperwork and greet any visitors who might stop by.

Laura was serving in a secretarial capacity on a temporary basis. She was one of those individuals to whom everyone was instantly attracted. A "people person," she exuded enthusiasm and a genuine sense of love and compassion for everyone she met. She had served the ministry well, especially in those aspects of her work which related to people. And although she made a concerted effort to maintain the day-to-day clerical tasks, those tasks paled when she compared them to the importance of ministering to people.

It was vital that I fulfill this particular speaking engagement. I found solace in the thought that the center would be quiet that day since classes were not in session. Perhaps Laura might make a dent in the huge stack of work. I reminded her of the long list of projects, encouraged her to make the best use of her time and hurried out the door.

"Lord," I prayed as I drove to my appointment, "there's so much that needs to be done in the office. You know how much Laura loves people. If anyone stops by, I know Laura will want to spend time with them. Please help her to concentrate and stay focused on the *important* tasks at hand."

Adding to my sense of pressure was the knowledge of a failed fund-raiser which had taken place the previous week. A great deal of time and energy had been spent organizing a city-wide car-wash-a-thon. The results had been a monumental disappointment! Rather than the $6,000 which we had expected to raise, our profit was only a few hundred. I wrestled with the weighty problem of our financial needs as I drove to the church where I was to speak.

Meanwhile, back at the office, my concern for Laura's time was indeed being realized. Laura later told me that an older gentleman, modestly dressed, had appeared at the center soon after I left and that she had greeted the stranger.

He quietly asked Laura if she had just a few minutes for "an old man." She gave the visitor a warm smile, took his arm and said, "Of course. Won't you please sit down?"

Over a cup of coffee, the gentleman explained to Laura that his wife, who had recently passed away, had felt a special attachment to the ministry of The Little

Light House and the children we served. He said she had spoken of it often. He wanted to come and meet those carrying out the ministry to the children who had so captured his wife's heart. Laura listened intently to his story.

The stranger wept as he spoke, still feeling the pain of his loss. Awhile later, apologizing for his tears and for taking so much of her time, he thanked Laura and asked if he might "come back later to see Mrs. Mitchell." Laura, of course, welcomed him to do so.

"One last thing," he said as he turned to leave. "Please say nothing to Mrs. Mitchell of my visit or my intention to come by later." Laura gave him her word that she wouldn't and kept her promise.

A few hours later, I was standing just outside my office and noticed a stranger enter the front door. He was a kindly-looking man.

I greeted him and introduced myself. He asked for a few moments of my time. "Of course," I responded as we moved toward my office. He told of his dear wife and her love for the special children of The Little Light House, just as he had explained to Laura earlier. My heart was moved with compassion as he wept and reflected on her life. Later, I showed him through the center.

As he prepared to leave, he turned and said, "I have a gift that my wife wanted The Little Light House to have. But before I delivered it, I needed to see if folks here would take time for an old man." With that, he pulled a check from his pocket and handed it to me. I looked in astonishment at the amount — $6,000! The very amount we had hoped to raise from the "washed out" car-wash-a-thon! My prayer had been answered. Indeed the Lord had kept Laura focused on what was really *important* and had delivered a treasured lesson to me in the process!

> Don't forget to be kind to strangers, for some who have done this have entertained angels without realizing it! (Hebrews 13:2)

25
God's Economy

In 1986, the oil business was suffering. Consequently, the Oklahoma economy was experiencing a dramatic slump. A number of large corporations which had previously supported local charities were shutting down. Many individuals hurt by the financial crunch were cutting back in their giving. Unfortunately, it was at this same time that the ministry was experiencing another rather significant growth spurt.

I began hearing words of caution and doubt from well-meaning friends and supporters. "A non-profit, tuition-free center like The Little Light House will never survive this blow to the Oklahoma economy," they would say.

I, too, wondered if the center could survive these "times." On the other hand, I reasoned, God is not — nor has He ever been — dependent upon the economy to accomplish His will. I yearned for God to demonstrate that truth to my world.

Staff members had heard what it had been like eight years before, when staff had voluntarily gone without "regular" paychecks. They, too, experienced it first-hand during that year.

Their faith was tried as they waited and prayed for adequate funds to cover their checks. The staff proved faithful during those difficult days, reaching out, ministering to the precious little ones God had placed in our care. When paychecks were delayed, they formed "staff commune grocery exchange lists" just as staff members had done years earlier. They encouraged one another and prayed for one another. Still, the months dragged by, bringing no relief to the financial drought.

"Please, Lord," I prayed. "Please send provision for us. I'm grateful that we can always pay our bills, but we need to pay the staff as well."

On some days, there was no income whatsoever. On other days, we had only enough to enable us to pay the bills and barely pay those staff members who needed their checks. Those with savings, or a spouse's salary or other income cut back on their expenses to a sacrificial degree and continued voluntarily to go without their paychecks.

By September of that year, several staff members had voluntarily gone without paychecks for more than three months. We needed $18,000 to pay them in full for earned wages. Another $12,000 was needed within days to keep all bills paid.

Judy, a dedicated educator on our staff, served as a constant source of encouragement as she consistently reminded me that the number of digits in those figures were irrelevant to God. Still I couldn't help but feel overwhelmed each time I thought about the scope of our need. My faith had been strengthened in previous years as I observed God work in ways I could never have dreamed of. I knew He could change our circumstances, yet I wondered why He seemed so slow to move in this instance.

Oftentimes, I found solace and comfort in pouring out my heart to God in the form of a letter.

One autumn day, I sat down in the quiet of my office and wrote –

> Lord, I don't know why you're allowing this long financial drought. I *do* know you work all things together for good for those who love you and are fitting into your plans! I *do* know you can change our income in an instant and I'm *sure* you must have good reason for withholding blessings.
>
> But, Lord, please send provision and financial relief soon. The staff have kept the faith. They are caring for one another. I'm concerned, once again, that they may not even have enough food to eat. Yet I hear no complaints. Please, Lord, please send provision soon.
>
> And, Lord, I've been hearing many say that The Little Light House will never survive this recession. So when you do provide, would you do so in such a way that it demonstrates to our world that you are not dependent upon the Oklahoma economy?
>
> And, there's another thing, Lord. Some people have the mistaken notion that our funds come as a result of our ability to persuade folks to give. So, if somehow you could please provide through someone who has no way of knowing our need. That way, Lord, no one can attribute it to anything I or anyone else has said or done.

I finished the letter, remembering again the exorbitant figure I was praying for. Thirty thousand dollars – what a staggering sum of money! Then I remembered the time when we had been in need of the same sum and a local church had called to tell us an individual had designated a gift of $15,000 to The Little Light House. They went on to say that the gift had been matched, bringing the total donation to $30,000! God is able and I knew when the timing was right, He would make provision for us, no matter what the sum!

The Bible tells us we have not, because we ask not. (See James 4:2.) Clearly, I had asked and had given the request over to Him and had trusted Him with our needs.

That same week, Linda, my assistant, took a call from an attorney requesting an appointment for me to come to his office to pick up a check. He explained that in 1978, one of his clients had named The Little Light House in her will. She had passed away in December of 1985, and her estate had been tied up in probate until September of 1986. Finally, his firm was ready to release the portion of her estate which had been willed to The Little Light House. The amount of the check was for $34,000!

As I drove back to the center with the check, I reflected on my prayer. I had asked God to please provide soon. Our answer came within the week. I had appealed to Him to provide through someone who had no way of knowing our need. The provision came from someone who had passed away before our need actually arose.

I petitioned God to provide in such a way that it would demonstrate to our world that His provision was not dependent upon our state's economy. He did exactly that! In 1978, He worked through a dear lady to make provision for the 1986 economy! What an answer to prayer! What an awesome God!

> O Lord my God, many and many a time you have done great miracles for us and we are ever in your thoughts. Who else can do such glorious things? No one else can be compared with you. There isn't time to tell of all your wonderful deeds. (Psalms 40:5)

26
Promised Land

It became more and more evident that God had a special plan for The Little Light House. Word of our commitment to quality, tuition-free services within a Christian environment continued to circulate among professionals in medical and educational fields. An increasing number of referrals were coming from professionals in the area. The population trend veered from the deaf-blind to those born with autism, spina bifida, cerebral palsy and Down's syndrome. Almost on a daily basis, we received calls from families wanting to enroll their children. Finally, reaching the maximum capacity our space would allow, we had had to establish a waiting list.

During this time, I couldn't help but recall the questions I had pondered in 1977, when I had wondered if God was calling us to prepare an "ark of ministry" for His beloved special children. And if so, if there would be a flood of children in the future in need of our services. At the time there was no evidence of need, much less a flood. Yet, now it seemed the flood waters were beginning to rise. And although it was heartbreaking to behold the tremendous needs of these children, I was in awe of our God who had anticipated their needs, years before they existed, and wouldn't allow us to close the doors that would later need to open wide to the "least of these."

Families were waiting up to three years to enroll their children, and our waiting list of over 100 children was still rising. Our board of directors was gravely concerned. We were at maximum capacity in the one-story church building which had originally afforded us more space than we ever imagined needing. Each year our host church had allowed us to occupy additional rooms in their educational wing, until finally there was no more room to expand. Speech therapists resorted to modifying a small bathroom into a therapy room. They practiced in this bathroom, as well as in a partitioned area of a hallway.

The small classrooms placed enormous restraints on the freedom of movement needed for therapy exercises, and the types of equipment which could be used.

We stretched as far as we dared, increasing the number of staff and volunteers, to serve as many students as possible in the cramped quarters. Time and again, we shifted furniture, seeking to find the best use of space.

Finally, we recognized the inevitable need for a permanent home for the center. For eleven years, we had occupied "borrowed" church space. Every Monday our staff of professionals put away Sunday school tables and chairs and set out therapy equipment, educational furniture and supplies. At one point, while occupying church space, our staff was moving ninety chairs twice a week. We were ready for a permanent home.

Our board sought the Lord in prayer. In no way did they want to deviate from God's perfect will for the ministry. It was a serious matter, considering the impact a building program could have on our day-today operations revenue. After extensive prayer and discussion, the senior members of the board remembered the time when correctly discerning the will of God might have made the difference between the continuance or the closing of the ministry.

Our board decided, once again, to ask God to *confirm* the direction they believed they were receiving from Him through a financial fleece.

In an effort to assure our staff of continued salaries, they asked God to make provision for adequate funding to cover all operating expenses through the end of the fiscal year, plus sufficient revenue to add two much-needed therapists to our staff. The total financial fleece amounted to $219,230.

By the targeted date, $219,240 had been received. God also confirmed His direction for us in numerous other ways, through Scripture, through a spirit of peace in us and through excellent counsel. Consequently, the therapists were hired and plans were established to begin reviewing paralleling facilities throughout the country. It was decided early on that the *entire* project would have to be completed on a debt-free basis. God had confirmed His direction for the center, and we intended to trust Him fully for His provision.

The building fund which had been established years before had increased slightly over the years, but it hardly made up the sum we needed. Our board communicated the existence of the fund to our supporters, as well as the need for a permanent home, and began seeking a permanent location.

For years, we had prayed for the perfect site. We prayed for a location equally distanced between two local universities which for years had provided practicum students and volunteers for our program. We dreamed of a plot of land next door to a church (so we could share parking), close to a park (for sunny-day picnics) and in close proximity to expressways to accommodate families in surrounding areas.

The very first location we looked at met every specification. It was a beautiful piece of land, set on a hill, right in the center of Tulsa. It was located across the street from a church and next door to one as well. The land was adjacent to a lovely park. The location at 36th and Yale was within one mile of major expressways. It was also perfectly centered between the two universities. This land was definitely worth praying about.

A cherished friend of mine who lived near the location had a prayer appointment with God every morning at 7:00 when she took a walk. I asked her if she would pray each day for The Little Light House to be able to purchase this land if, of course, it was the will of God for the ministry to have it. She agreed.

Weeks later, we learned that this property we found to be so ideal was caught up in some legal entanglements and would not be available for purchase for some time. Still, we believed God had the perfect location for us, and Mike Brady, Little Light House board chairman and the board's land and building committee chairman, was just the one to find it. He led his committee with enthusiasm and passion as they viewed one piece of real estate after another.

It took such a man to lead the committee in their relentless search. Property was viewed countless times, sometimes prices were negotiated, but one site after another faded from view as each was pursued and then abandoned for various, but valid reasons.

At times, I felt impatient. Since the founding of the center, I had dreamed of the day God's special children in Tulsa would have a beautiful facility, tailor-made to meet their needs. The trips we had made to leading agencies throughout the United States and Canada had convinced me of the value and the need for quality facilities for disabled children.

Two long years of searching for a building site passed. It seemed we were no closer than we had been when we first began praying and searching. We certainly had not seen anything to compare to the first land we had viewed. It was the only piece of property we ever saw that met all of our specifications.

Then one day I received a mysterious and totally unexpected call. The man's voice on the other end of the line was deep and strong. I recognized his name as a man I knew from church. After the usual amenities, he blurted out a question which had obviously been weighing on his mind for days.

"Marcia, tell me — did God tell you that The Little Light House is to be located at 36th and Yale?"

I was stunned. That was where we had viewed the very first piece of property two years earlier, the only land that had met all the criteria we had set forth. My voice shook slightly as I finally responded, "Why do you ask?"

His response was intriguing. It seems he had great plans for this land he owned. He had worked feverishly on zoning and had spent thousands of dollars on architectural renderings. His problems began when the recurring thought kept going through his mind that The Little Light House was to be located on his cherished piece of property!

Being a smart businessman and feeling that our organization likely couldn't pay him what the property was worth, he tried to dismiss the thought, but to no avail. Finally, he decided to talk to his wife. He reasoned that she certainly understood the value of the property. Surely she would support his reasoning. Her assurance would ease his mind and allow him to forget the notion that The Little Light House should occupy his land!

He shared his thoughts with her, pointing out the financial benefits of developing the property in other ways. When he finished, she asked only one question. "But, Ralph, what if God wants The Little Light House to be there?"

Frustrated, he decided to approach his father who was also a businessman. Again, he reviewed the investment options available to him. After all, a ministry could never pay top dollar for the property. To his dismay, his father's response matched that of his wife's!

In desperation, he sought the counsel of the financial advisor at his bank. This time he decided not to mention The Little Light House at all. Rather, he talked only about the development options available. When he finished, Jim, his advisor, said, "Ralph, I'm on the land and building committee for The Little Light House. Would you consider selling this piece of property to The Little Light House?"

Ralph was dumbfounded. Finally, he threw up his hands and said, "Okay, God. If you want The Little

Light House on this land, so be it!" He called me within the week.

As soon as I hung up the phone from talking to him, I couldn't wait to call my friend who had been so willing to pray for that piece of property. I wondered if she would remember our conversation or my request for her to pray two years before. When I reached her, I asked excitedly if she remembered when I had asked her to pray for the property at 36th and Yale. "Of course," she responded, "I never *stopped* praying for it. Was I supposed to?"

Tears stung my eyes. "O Lord, you're an awesome God," I whispered as I hung up the receiver at the close of our conversation. "Only you could bring us back full circle and raise up this very piece of land — our 'promised land,' bringing it to our attention in such a way."

I drove to the beautiful hill at 36th and Yale. I parked my car, rolled down my window, and felt the gentle breeze against my face. "Lord, it's everything we've prayed for, and just the spot these children deserve."

It truly was the perfect "promised land," and there was no doubt we had a Divine Realtor!

> And we are sure of this, that he will listen to us whenever we ask him for anything in line with his will. And if we really know he is listening when we talk to him and make our requests, then we can be sure that he will answer us. (1 John 5:14-15)

Obviously, God had moved on the landowner's heart to sell the land we had so yearned to buy. When the property was finally free of legal encumbrances, it seemed evident that God was directing us to proceed.

Only one problem remained. Our board was committed to carrying through with the entire project on a debt-free basis, and the difference between the cost of the land and our building fund balance was in the hundreds of thousands of dollars.

Once again, we turned to God. We had never conducted a major funds campaign. We knew nothing of how to go about the process. We prayed fervently for divine guidance and for favor from men who were in a position to help us.

The Mary K. Chapman Foundation is a locally based foundation which had been used of God countless times throughout the history of The Little Light House. Once again, God worked through their kind *and* generous representative. He was enthusiastic about our ministry and the project we were embarking on!

He met and communicated with us on an ongoing basis to provide invaluable counsel to us. He coached us in the preparation of grant applications and proposals which were then submitted to other foundations. (Oftentimes, they were accompanied by a good word about us from him.)

The building fund slowly began to increase. Other foundations, individuals, corporations and civic clubs caught our vision and they, too, began to add to the "building coffers." Still we fell far short of the total amount needed.

We continued to pray. There was little else we could do. Some advised us to get a loan for the remaining amount, but our board stood firm to their conviction that there could be no debt. Seven days out, we lacked $30,201. Four days later, $25,000 was donated by an anonymous donor. The day before the closing, the last of the remaining sum we needed was provided. On the day of the closing, as we signed the last legal document giving us deed to the land, there was no question in our minds that we had witnessed another twentieth-century miracle!

> For since the world began no one has seen or heard of such a God as ours, who works for those who wait for him! (Isaiah 64:4)

27
Master Coordinator

We finally had taken possession of our "promised land." The provision of such a significant sum of money had seemed to us to be equivalent to the parting of the Red Sea for the Israelites. Our faith was at an all-time high! Still, we had a long way to go before God's special children would have the ideal special education facility we so yearned to provide for them.

Locating and contracting the right expertise to design and construct the building *seemed* to be an ominous task in itself. We could only guess the cost of such a venture. The purchase of the land had depleted our building fund. Once again, we turned to our heavenly Father. Once again — He proved faithful. Slowly but surely, the fund began to grow.

Jean, my loyal friend and invaluable cohort in charge of grants and endowments for The Little Light House, prayed fervently and worked feverishly on new grant proposals for construction funds. Meanwhile our board began the process of selecting an architect. They interviewed a number of architects and finally narrowed the list down to four firms. I was then asked to continue with the interviewing process and select the one I felt would be most qualified for the task.

The day came for the interviews. I asked each firm the same list of questions. I was particularly interested in knowing why they felt qualified to design so unique a building project. Each of the first three firms provided impressive answers as they presented portfolios of their work and verbalized a wide diversification of past projects. "Lord," I prayed after interviewing the first three, "please reveal to me the firm that is *your* choice for this project!"

Finally the last firm representative was to be interviewed. "Tell me, Jim," I began, "what have you done in the past that would qualify you to design such a unique facility as ours?"

Jim thought for a moment and then spoke, "Quite honestly, I'm not sure I *am* qualified for the task. I'd have to be on my knees, praying every inch of the way."

Peace flooded my spirit. "Oh, thank you, Lord," I prayed silently. "Now I know which one to recommend – the one committed to relying on your divine assistance!"

An additional architectural firm was contracted to work jointly with Jim Stanton and his firm in designing and overseeing the entire construction project. Working together, the firms offered economical solutions without harming the integrity of the facility.

Hundreds of hours were spent studying and determining the facility needs of The Little Light House. Ideas which we collected from out-of-state visits were analyzed. Therapists and teachers were interviewed by Jim as he diligently sought to accurately define the components of a model special education facility fully customized to accomodate the young children within our unique program.

Once the architectural renderings were in order, cost projections were calculated. These figures were then compared with the building funds in hand at the time and those we anticipated receiving prior to breaking ground. When we realized that our funds fell far short of the cost projections, the plans would go back to the drawing boards to be modified in order to fit within our building allowance. This process was repeated time and again. Adding to the complexity of the situation was the fluctuating cost of materials. At times we felt the process would never end. I remembered the same feeling from times past, but I also remembered God's faithfulness!

Finally, twenty-eight months after we purchased the land, by the grace and power of God, adequate funds had been received into our building fund to allow us to begin construction of the permanent homesite for The Little Light House! God had worked through precious and valuable instruments like Jean, a godly board of dedicated individuals and many others, but each one would be the first to say that it was God's power at work within them that brought the ministry to that point!

On July 27, 1989, The Little Light House broke ground and construction began on a beautiful, permanent facility. During the winter months, God held the bad weather at bay, allowing our general contractor to progress rapidly into the new year. Though the process had seemed agonizingly slow for years, suddenly the project was moving more rapidly than I had ever dreamed.

As completion appeared on the horizon, decisions and choices emerged that needed attention. Interior colors had to be selected to blend with various finishes as well as with our colorful equipment. This required the expertise of an interior designer — expertise we did not have and could not afford!

One evening a box was delivered to me from the architectural firm. It contained tile, paint and carpet samples and had a set of forms to be filled out indicating our decor selections. I was at a loss! The thought of decorating our own personal residence had been challenging to me. I couldn't imagine planning the decor for a 22,000-square-foot facility! Again I asked for the Lord's help. I prayed for the Lord to send an expert to offer assistance or skills *soon!*

The next morning I received a call from a member of our Little Light House Auxiliary. She wanted to know who was doing our interior design work for our new facility.

"Oh, Vicky, I'm so glad you asked. I have no one, and they've just delivered the most formidable-looking box of samples and forms to me! I've been praying for God to send us qualified help."

"Well, maybe that's why I've been feeling a nudge to call you!" she quickly responded. "Perhaps you don't know I do interior decorating. In fact, I've just completed designing a doctor's office complex. Maybe I can help you!" I was exuberant!

The next morning Vicky picked up the samples and we discussed general ideas for the interior. It was evident from the start that Vicky was moved by God to volunteer for this enormous task and she dedicated herself untiringly to the effort without any financial compensation whatsoever!

We were barely over that hurdle when I received a phone call from a long-time friend and Rotarian. Tom came to the point quickly, explaining that the Rotarians of Tulsa were preparing to celebrate their seventy-fifth anniversary. The members had decided to commemorate their anniversary by donating $50,000 to a local charity project. He asked if there was a project relating to our new building that they could commit to.

Immediately our playgrounds came to mind. We had dreams for several play areas. The dreams included carefully selected plants which would give off an aroma that would allow our blind children to identify which playground they were on. Our staff had also dreamed of adaptive playground equipment that even our children with low muscle tone could benefit from and play on. Our ideas were endless.

Excitedly, I told him about the project, hoping he would take an interest in the idea. He did! However, he stopped me short when he said, "I assume you have playground blueprints."

"Why no, Tom. We have the ideas and dreams in our head. We have nothing on paper."

"How quickly can you get some renderings?" he asked. "I don't even know where to go to for such plans, but I'll do my best," I responded, wondering to myself where I would even start.

He told me he would go ahead and discuss the project with his committee if I would start working on the playground plans. Soon after, I called Jim, our architect, who by this time had demonstrated quite a dedication to our project and to The Little Light House ministry.

"Jim, you're not going to believe this, but we have an opportunity to get our playgrounds donated." My words came fast as I quickly recapped the Rotarians' offer. "We need plans, though. If we give you our ideas, could you put some plans together?"

Jim expressed his concern regarding his lack of training and qualifications in the area of landscape design, but he expressed a willingness to at least get the plans started.

As soon as he began to put time and effort into the project, he realized he was out of his field of expertise and needed qualified assistance. He asked one of his associates if she knew of anyone who might have expertise in the area. Though she didn't, she agreed to contact a friend, Greg Warren, who was a landscape architect with the city.

After explaining the nature of the need to Greg, she asked if he might be willing to assist Jim in the playground project.

"What agency is this for?" he asked.

"It's a place called The Little Light House. It's a center for —." Before she could continue, he broke in.

"You're kidding," he said. "My wife and I just enrolled our little girl there last week! Tell Jim to turn this project over to me. I'll take care of it!"

Once again, God had just the right person at the right hour. Within a short time, the landscape architect had the plans completed.

The Rotarians did decide to adopt the project and provided the funds to launch our dream playground. Their generous gift of $50,000 allowed complete construction of four main play areas and allowed us to purchase numerous, brightly colored pieces of special play equipment. The playground has provided untold hours of play therapy, making the outdoors an extension of the classroom. Their benevolent-minded spirit set the stage for others, like Ronald McDonald Children's Charity and Farmers Insurance Group, to follow suit by contributing wonderful additions to our playground heaven.

God continued to coordinate people and circumstances together in His perfect timing, and always in such a way that it was very obviously *His* handiwork.

As we came closer to completion, the construction superintendent needed to know whether or not we planned to install automatic doors for the front lobby area. We desperately needed these doors for our special children and their wheelchairs. However, we still lacked the $15,000 needed to include them in our plans.

Jean received a call from the construction superintendent informing us he would have to know our decision about the doors no later than the next day.

She had barely lifted her hand from the receiver when another call came through. This time it was the president of a foundation which had already pledged $150,000 to our facility. He was calling to commit an additional $50,000 to our building project! In addition to that, he asked her if there might be a project relating to the building which would cost around $14,000 or $15,000 for which he personally could designate some stock money. Again, God's timing was perfect. We had the funds *just* in time to approve the automatic doors.

The moving date drew closer, and the building construction was still debt-free! Matters which had at one time seemed like distant concerns suddenly loomed ever nearer. Due to our preoccupation with the construction project, there were needs which we hadn't taken time to think about and for which we certainly had no funds. One such need was for office furniture, tables and chairs. The churches which had housed us in the past had always allowed us to use their office furniture. We owned only two folding chairs, a few tables and a few antiquated desks.

We had just begun to concern ourselves with this matter when a call came in from the spouse of one of our staff members. He explained that his company was moving. They were planning to purchase new furniture and wondered if we could use their present furniture. By this time, Vicky had selected the colors for the center — mauve, teal, and soft shades of gray. Having seen God work in such wonderful ways in the past, it came as no surprise to us that the colors of the donated furniture blended in perfectly.

Other provisions revealed the hand of our *Master Coordinator*. For example, one evening I counted the number of bathrooms in our new facility. Including all the sinks in the children's bathrooms, they totaled twenty-five! I wondered how in the world we were going to fill all those soap dispensers. Always before, we had only a few bathrooms for which to supply soap, and besides, through a tradition called "blessing baskets," friends supplied ordinary items like Kleenex and bar soap on an ongoing basis. But, these dispensers required a special kind of anti-bacterial liquid soap!

"Lord," I prayed, "I know this sounds like a strange request when we've been asking for $100,000 grants and $15,000 automatic doors, but I'm concerned about how we are going to fill all those soap dispensers on a regular basis. They're already installed now."

That same week, the husband of one of our volunteers stopped by to talk to me. His wife had noticed the dispensers and mentioned them to him since his company "just happened" to sell the kind of liquid soap they required. With a smile, he offered to provide all the soap we needed for the dispensers along with many other needed supplies!

After my brief conversation, my heart overflowed again with praise. "O Lord, you're an awesome God! Thank you for all the wonderful people who allow you to work through them." The list of the folks God raised up to perform various tasks goes on and on. The same friend who had once supplied donuts for us acquired countless items that met our needs, ranging from garbage disposals to carpet sweepers. One pupil's grandparents donated wallpaper and the labor to hang it. Another friend re-upholstered our old furniture for us. Still another parent donated all the professional interior signs.

Staff, parents and grandparents rallied together to lay the sod which had been donated by a benevolent company. Designated gifts came in for a sprinkler system, and another company donated all the labor to install it. A landscape architect donated his expertise to design a landscape plan for us.

Kitchen appliances, paintings and plants appeared out of the blue. Lockers which had been planned for our volunteers had to be cut out of our budget. Yet weeks later, an oil company that didn't know we had even hoped for lockers sent over a unit of fifty, which they no longer needed! They were almost identical to the ones we had originally intended to order! Another oil company donated 110 place settings of silverware.

The list of contributors was extensive *and* all divinely coordinated. It was glorious to behold the giving spirit of such a caring community.

Finally the day we had dreamed of, worked towards and prayed for came – April 7, 1990. The sun was shining brightly as men and women from civic groups and other friends from throughout the city gathered to help move the entire Little Light House facility. There was a light and celebrant spirit evident in the entire crew that day. We truly had something to celebrate!

God had led us to our "promised land," and He had been faithful to plan our steps and then serve as the Master Coordinator every step of the way!

"Who can say but that God has brought you into the palace for just such a time as this?" (Esther 4:14b)

28
State-of-the-*Heart* Curriculum

April 30, 1990. It was a milestone day. It marked the culmination of seventeen and a half years of miracles. It was the first day of school at The Little Light House in our spacious, new permanent homesite.

Over 100 volunteers had assisted with the massive move. Following that major undertaking, our staff had worked feverishly for twenty-one days – unpacking boxes, stocking cabinets, decorating bulletin boards, setting out teaching aids and positioning therapy equipment – in preparation for the day when our children would arrive for their first day of classes.

Emotions ran high as our staff gathered at daybreak for a time of prayer and praise. As we did so, I couldn't help reflecting on a cool autumn day in 1972 when Kristi and I and our first five volunteers gathered in the same way to start our day. Far more voices joined in on this morning, however, as choruses of "Praise God From Whom All Blessings Flow" echoed through the halls.

Following our staff's morning devotional, we asked God's guidance, protection and blessing on the day. Moments later, teachers hurried to their classrooms to make last-minute preparations before the children began arriving.

By 8:00 AM there was a buzz of excitement. Broad smiles adorned the faces of volunteers as they stepped into the new building and were greeted with hugs from a welcoming crew of staff members. Afterwards, parents pushed small wheelchairs bearing wide-eyed children through the front entrance as large, automatic glass doors seemed to open as if by magic. Other eager children worked hard to make their way independently, relying only on their walkers for assistance as their parents followed close behind. Some held tightly to the hands of their moms and dads. Then there were those who raced through the entrance into the arms of their beloved "Wally," a retired Englishman who had devoted the past fourteen years of his life to "the wee ones."

One by one, each made his way down the halls to their new, colorful classrooms. A special education staff of teachers, teaching assistants, therapists and a nurse had carefully and lovingly planned for the day, keeping the schedule simple and relaxed to allow the children to adjust to their new surroundings.

After the children were all settled in, I led the parents on a tour through the facility. Each classroom was alive with activity. Volunteers lovingly led children through programs which were painstakingly prescribed and clearly outlined on activity cards that matched instructions with the appropriate equipment.

The parents looked on with pride at their own little ones as they anticipated the learning and growing that would take place in their beautiful new school. Most of them had waited three years for their child to be enrolled, due to the length of our waiting list. They didn't take lightly the privilege of having their child enrolled at The Little Light House.

Soon classes were in full swing, the parents were on their way, and I returned to my office. As I sat down at my desk, my heart welled up with emotion — as I let the fact sink in that our dream had finally become a reality. The words Sheryl and I had voiced so many years ago came quickly to mind: "Wouldn't it be wonderful if Tulsa could have its own special school for these children?"

Yes, we had dreamed. But never had we imagined all God had in store along the way. The miracles, the milestones — all had been a part of His plan. Only by His grace and power did His plan unfold. It was finally a divine reality! And as a result, those of us who had witnessed its development had been strengthened spiritually. To God be the glory!

* * *

A Dream for the Future

Frequently, we are asked where God is leading The Little Light House. At the time of this writing we are still seeking His direction. However, we *can* say we believe the day may come when God will lead our staff to reach out to other parts of the country and perhaps even to other nations to provide training opportunities for those who would minister to physically and mentally challenged children. Our hearts go out to the "least of these" who, in some parts of our globe, are not allowed to learn and in some cases may even be allowed to die simply because they aren't viewed as "normal." We believe there is a way for the people of these nations to be given the vision, skills and knowledge they need to help such children develop the potential that lies within them. And as we teach and as we train others, our hope and our dream is that in that process, the world will be gently and lovingly exposed to the light of a risen Savior – a Savior who offers a gift far more valuable than a physical healing, a Savior who promises eternal life.

> Let your light so shine before men, that they may see your good works, and glorify your Father which is in heaven. (Matthew 5:16, KJV)

Epilogue

I've been amazed as I have retraced God's hand through the formative years of The Little Light House. The masterful way in which He interweaves our trials and triumphs into His sovereign plan and purpose is awesome to say the least.

I was equally intrigued as I reflected on the circumstances and experiences of my own personal life. For what appeared at one time to be unrelated parts of a puzzle *were,* in fact, the very pieces God needed to picture for me the calling He had planned for my life. It all began when I was a small child.

It was an evening I'll always remember. I was only seven at the time, but the memory is etched in my mind. Friends and neighbors were pouring into our home. Everyone was wiping tears from their eyes.

My parents had been away with my little four-and-one-half-year-old sister who had been hospitalized with a serious illness. She had been sick much of her young life and had been hospitalized numerous times, but she always came home. My older sister and I adored her and had been eagerly awaiting her return once again. But that wasn't to be.

Instead, my parents returned home without her. It was gently explained to us that Kathie wouldn't be coming home this time. She was gone. She had gone to live with Jesus — in heaven.

All evening, I felt sick. I wanted to cry, but the tears didn't seem to come. I kept thinking about Jesus and the pictures I had seen of Him in Sunday school — always with lots of children surrounding Him. Why, I wondered, did He have to take our golden-haired Kathie, when He had all those other children to play with?

Bitterness took root in those thoughts, and quietly through the years, my heart grew indifferent to the person of Jesus Christ.

Not long before my eighth birthday, we moved — not far away, only about a mile, in fact. Our former two-story brick home held too many memories for my parents, I suppose. They were special memories, but they brought pain.

A new little neighbor friend, who was close to my age, filled the void in my life, and we became friends. She was blind. I was lonely. She was strong, bright, independent and extraordinarily gifted. I was in awe of her talent. She taught me how to play songs on the piano by ear. I read stories to her on the back porch step.

She introduced me to her piano teacher, and we, too, became friends. I was intrigued with the fact that the teacher could always tell if I tried switching the proper fingering on a piano piece even though he, too, was totally blind.

By the time I reached my twelfth birthday, I had adjusted fairly well to the loss of Kathie, or so I thought. Then one day I ran across a little book that brought all the memories of her rushing back like a torrent.

It was written by Dale Evans Rogers. It's the story of her little baby girl, Robin Elizabeth Rogers, who also came into the world with a handicapping condition like Kathie, and passed away at the age of two.

Dale believes God sent Robin on a two-year mission to their household to strengthen them spiritually and to draw them closer together in the knowledge and love and fellowship of God.

When I finished the small book, the floodgates of my emotions opened wide and all the bitterness, confusion and resentment over Kathie's death that I had stored up for years, rushed through my whole being in the form of heaving sobs. The realization that God had a purpose for Kathie's life swept through me, and I wondered if I was too late to benefit from the message that I was sure God wanted me to receive through her life – the message that He loved me and had a purpose for me to fulfill.

It was at that point that I entered into a personal relationship with Jesus Christ and purposed to understand the mission He had for my life. The experience had such an impact on me, I even developed a heart's desire to one day enter the mission field.

When I was fourteen, we moved miles away from my childhood friend, and I rarely got to see her after that, though she has always had a special place in my heart.

By the time I reached my senior year in high school, I had developed new aspirations to become a speech pathologist. Kathie had been the victim of a cleft palate and had significant speech problems. I thought it would be wonderful to help "special" children like her.

A high school advisor discouraged me from pursuing that vocation, however, and as a result of his counsel, I pursued a degree in speech and drama instead. It was an area of study I had enjoyed in high school. College was no exception. I fell in love with theater arts. The highlight of my college years was when I was given the lead role as Helen Keller in "The Miracle Worker." For three months, I researched her life story and studied the world of the blind. Under a blindfold and with cotton stuffed in my ears, I took long walks, made my bed, went to the grocery store, to campus parties and even out on dates.

The insights I gained in the process proved invaluable a couple of years later when I began teaching speech and drama and discovered I had a totally blind student in my classroom.

I knew all of these experiences would make a lasting imprint on my heart, mind and soul. I didn't know to what extent, however, until years later when I heard the words, "Your baby will be, at best, legally blind."

Reflecting on those early years, when the Lord led us to establish The Little Light House, I marvel over how God has taken the puzzle pieces of my life and fit them together to enable me to accomplish His purpose for my life.

There's no doubt that He desires to put those pieces together for each and every one of His children. As we yield our lives to Him, we give Him the power to bring purpose and meaning from the mountaintops and valleys of our lives.

He has put the pieces together for Missy as well. Today she is a mature young woman with a call on her life to a contemporary Christian music ministry. She interweaves contemporary Christian music with her testimony as she sings and shares with young and old alike about the challenges and joys of her life. People seem especially ministered to when she shares about a time in her life when she began asking why she had been born visually impaired.

"Darlin'," I softly told her one day when she was feeling especially low, "you can ask *why* for the rest of your life, and it will only lead to pain and despair. But if you will ask God *how* – *how* He can use the circumstances of your life for good, you will find joy and victory!" It was a lesson God had impressed on my heart years before. The lesson has proven true for her as well, and I believe it holds true for all God's children.

And now my prayer is that the truth of this principle might penetrate the hearts of those who read our story. For as we allow our heavenly Father to turn our tears into triumph, and our valleys into victories, such miracle transformations will become milestones in our walk with the Master.

And we know that all that happens to us is working for our good if we love God and are fitting into his plans. (Romans 8:28)

MILESTONES & MIRACLES